Physioeconomics

Physioeconomics

The Basis for Long-Run
Economic Growth

Philip M. Parker

The MIT Press
Cambridge, Massachusetts
London, England

This book was set in Book Antigua by Icon Group International, Inc. using Microsoft Word 2000.

Printed and bound in the United States of America.

Library of Congress Cataloging-in-Publication Data

Parker, Philip M., 1960-
  Physioeconomics: the basis for long-run economic
  growth / Philip Parker.
      p. cm.
  Includes bibliographical references and index.
  ISBN 0-262-16194-X
  1. Economic development. 2. Physics. I. Title.

HB74.P49 P37 2000
339'.01 — dc21   00-021973

Contents

Preface and Acknowledgments

The goal of this book is to summarize and introduce the reader to the notion that certain physical laws and physiological concepts may prove useful in explaining both microeconomic and macroeconomic behaviors, especially as these might vary from country to country. Starting from the fact that humans are homeotherms by nature, this book mostly considers the effects of *heat transfer*, or thermodynamics, and the workings of the hypothalamus on certain economic fundamentals: utility and consumption. The research presented here indicates that individual utility systematically varies from one country to another as predicted by models of physics-based physiology. Enough empirical research from a variety of disciplines appears to confirm this finding so as to merit more general attention. This observation will be of most relevance to persons interested in understanding why long-run economic growth and behavior across countries will remain divergent. Poverty measurement issues and policy implications make this idea topical.

As with all interdisciplinary work, a careful balance between depth and breadth of coverage is required. To increase readability, many mathematical definitions have been placed in end notes. Further supporting information is provided in ample references which are offered to compensate for space limitations. Though most of the data relied upon for various figures and tables are in the public domain, please feel free to email requests for data used in this book to phil.parker@insead.fr or pmparker@ucsd.edu.

Organization

The first chapter begins with a review of the various explanations of growth including economic geography. The most persistent of geographic factors is the *equatorial paradox*. Observed by various thinkers throughout modern history, the closer a country is to the equator, the more likely it will have lower than average consumption per capita. Today, some seventy percent of the variances in income per capita across countries can be explained by absolute latitude. Supporting eighteenth-century predictions of Montesquieu, the paradox may be a telltale sign of certain physics-based physiological mechanisms at work. The second chapter summarizes certain empirical regularities found in various cross-country measures of development. In particular, the existence of a certain form of spatial correlation in international economic data is noted — an issue related to the paradox. Chapters 3 and 4 present conceptual building blocks from physics and physiology required to establish the notion of homeostatic utility. Chapter 5 explains how both physics and physiology require that utility functions take on specific functional forms, unlike those traditionally used in microeconomics.

Chapter 6 describes how homeostatic utility functions imply kinked consumption functions that must systematically vary from one country to another. Growth is theorized to take on a particular form of spatial correlation quite different from neighborhood effects. Rational utility maximization will thus lead to variances in consumption in line with the equatorial paradox. Experimental, time series, and cross-sectional empirical evidence is then provided to support this explanation. Predictable differences in steady-state behaviors are suggested by data reported for key consumption items that make up a substantial portion of income in both low- and high-income countries. In doing so, physical factors are argued to dominate alternative explanations of the paradox. The paradox explained, chapter 7 then suggests a number of measures of economic performance upon which forecasts of growth or traditional modeling can be based. In essence, a country's performance is gauged not by its absolute level of income or consumption, but rather by how far it is from a *homeostatic* steady state governed by, for lack of a better term, *physioeconomics*. Countries closer to their homeostatic steady states will grow slower than those farther away, even though they might have lower levels of consumption. Policy implications are then discussed in light of the fact that not all countries will converge to the same consumption steady state.

Chapter 8 ventures to make long-run predictions implied by utility maximization and the liberalization of markets. The predictions cover longevity (infant mortality, life expectancy), literacy, demography (fertility rates, birth rates, net reproduction rates, population growth rates), migration, income, and consumption.

The reader versed in traditional exogenous or endogenous models of growth will note that the incorporation of physics and physiology into theories of growth requires that emphasis be placed on the demand side: variances in utilities derived from consumption and the realization of consumption desires. Aggregate income, savings, investment, technology, entrepreneurship, production, and outputs per worker are thus considered endogenous to or driven by these more fundamental principles affecting variances in utility.

Acknowledgments

This book has benefited from a number of persons who have provided feedback, data, and technical advice. In addition to my colleagues at INSEAD and the University of California, San Diego, thanks are owed to participants in lectures and research presentations made at the Graduate School of Business at Stanford University, the Sloan School of Management at MIT, the School of Business of Columbia

University, and the Hautes Ecoles Commerciales. Constructive feedback and some of the data reported were obtained from persons at the World Bank, the International Monetary Fund and other participants in an INSEAD-Harvard-Stanford executive development program. Numerous sessions for McKinsey & Company on globalization also proved beneficial. Special thanks are owed to the libraries at the Hong Kong University of Science and Technology, the Sloan School of Management, INSEAD, and the Biomedical and Medical Libraries at the University of California, San Diego which gave me access to valuable collections. Thanks are also owed to Janine Adler and James Parker who made technical suggestions covering certain topics in physics and physiology. Nader Tavassoli and Miklos Sarvary have been critical sounding boards over the last few years. I am also grateful for encouraging comments from Reinhard Angelmar, Gilles Laurent, Donald Lehmann, John D.C. Little and Jordan Louviere. Thanks are owed for editorial assistance given by The MIT Press, Joelle Fabert, Erin Reeser, and Michaela Monahan. All errors are mine. Most thanks are owed to Claire, Paul and Régine for letting me invest some family time in this venture. Funding came from the Research and Development Committee of INSEAD, the members of which are owed much gratitude.

1   Introduction

By nature, men are nearly alike; by practice they get to be wide apart.

—Confucius

In his Nobel Prize address in December 1993, Robert Fogel conjectured that a link may exist between long-run economic growth and fundamental principles in physics and physiology (1994, p. 385):

> Recent findings in the biomedical area call attention to what may be called the thermodynamic and physiological factors in economic growth. Although largely neglected by theorists of both the "old" and the "new" growth economics, these factors can easily be incorporated into standard growth models.

This book takes Fogel's observations seriously. While he found that "a firm assessment of the physiological contribution to economic growth is not yet possible" (p. 368), I nevertheless attempt to introduce here the notion that strong and rather persistent relationships between physics-based physiology and economics may come to dominate explanations of economic growth.

Exploring how principles from the natural sciences might be important to economics requires a certain level of curiosity and patience on the part of the reader. The mere notion that traces of predictable economic growth might be related to hormones and neurotransmitters can be met with skepticism. The interdisciplinary nature of this conjecture requires that one proceeds with caution. This is especially important to avoid over simplification and, worse, hastily concluding that geographic, racial, or cultural differences are being masked in deterministic physiological jargon. A casual glance at a table or graph may lead to such conclusions. Nor should one leap to the conclusion that countries are destined to low performance based on infallible axioms from physics. The evidence presented indicates that race or culture (in the sense used by Max Weber) have no role in long-run growth processes. Furthermore, two countries with radically different development paths can achieve similar levels of economic performance or well-being, if these are properly measured.

The integration of physics and physiology into economics would be arcane if it were not for a well-recognized though particularly problematic paradox: *the equatorial paradox*, or what has recently been called the equatorial grand canyon. When a single exogenous variable, in this case a country's absolute latitude, explains up to 70 percent of the cross-country variances in income per capita, some explanation is required. Lacking proper resolution, discussions of optimal growth strategies and forecasts of long-run economic growth prove hazardous. This has been an especially sensitive issue for countries located in the tropics, where forecasts of growth have proven most difficult (Temple and Johnson 1998, p. 966). This book presents a physics-based physiological explanation of the paradox and long-run economic growth in general.[1] Adding such a perspective to current theories may lead to better evaluations of economic policies, measures of performance, and predictions of progress.

Standing Explanations of Growth

A number of factors surely affect the level of economic prosperity within and across countries. Those previously studied include social capital, capability, or infrastructure (Knack and Keefer 1997, Hall and Jones 1999, Temple and Johnson 1998), the exploitation of one class vis-à-vis another (McDermott 1997), international commodity flows (Ventura 1997), intellectual property rights enforcement (Tornell 1997), democracy or political regimes (Barro 1996, Minier 1998, Durham 1999), external shocks (Startz 1998), the diffusion of technology (Barro and Sala-i-Martin 1997), openness to trade and investment (Ben-David and Loewy 1998), technology and entrepreneurship (Aghion and Howitt 1998, Howitt and Aghion 1998, Basu and Weil 1998), physical and human capital (Galor and Tsiddon 1997, Judson 1998), labor involvement in agriculture

(Humphries and Knowles 1998), and a variety of other factors leading to poverty traps (Azariadis 1996).

These and many more structural, institutional, and environmental factors also have been identified in the literature on economic development (Todaro 1997, and Landau et al. 1996). On a global basis, the most persistent and difficult factors to model are geographic and cultural. In his opening thoughts in *The Wealth of Nations*, Adam Smith (1776) discusses the limits of a country's wealth as being bounded by its "soil, climate, or extent of territory." Following various other classical thinkers, this school of thought had its heyday in the early twentieth century. Alfred Marshall, in his *Principles of Economics*, noted that the Thames River "has added more to the wealth of England than all its canals, and perhaps even its railroads."[2] To this school, natural factor endowments include minerals, soil quality, access to fresh water, floodplains, coastlines or deep harbors, historical access to wild grains or large mammals that can easily be farmed or domesticated, the presence or absence of disease carrying vectors, forgiving climates, and strategic location. After wallowing for more than sixty years, this school has found late twentieth century advocates, including economic historians (e.g., David Landes, professor emeritus from Harvard University), economic geographers (e.g., Jeffery Sachs from Harvard University, Paul Krugman from MIT) and biogeographers (e.g., Jared Diamond of UCLA).

Their work points to a number of geographic, historical, institutional, and cultural "path dependencies" that are difficult if not impossible to ignore, especially to development economists and humanitarian workers in the field. The reasoning starts with the observation that all countries are not created equal. Some countries are poor because they have started with nothing, except everything that might inhibit economic growth (e.g., Sub-Saharan African nations almost always come to mind). Wealth, for others, has come from the luck of being able to start from highly diversified or benevolent geographic settings. A large portion of Kuwait's wealth, it is argued, is not determined by its political economy, but rather from its luck of the draw. Modern models of economic growth, which do not dwell on resource differences, will often split samples into "oil producing" and "non oil producing" countries—an implicit acknowledgment of resource-based effects on growth.[3]

Economic history has shown, however, that many of the effects of resource-based growth are ephemeral. Depletion, changes in technologies, changes in trade routes, and competition have consistently contributed to the elimination of resource-based growth. Furthermore, the wealth endowment of a given resource does not eliminate variance. Many countries are rich in oil or minerals (or natural location), but substantial variances in income remain across these resource-rich countries (e.g., compare Nigeria to Norway). Similarly, certain countries with few of these factor endowments have acquired high levels of income and consumption.

The Equatorial Paradox

Of all of the geographic factors, one shows tenacious persistence: latitude. Economists have long observed systematic differences in income using this simple metric (hereafter referred to in absolute value). For all countries without a strategic location or a natural endowment with arbitrage value (e.g., excluding Singapore, Hong Kong, Brunei), the facts are hard to ignore. Galbraith (1951, p. 693) observed: "[If] one marks off a belt a couple of thousand miles in width encircling the earth at the equator, one finds within it *no* developed countries."

This paradox has recently been noted in Hall and Jones (1999), Landes (1998), Norhhaus (1994), Parker (1995), Theil and Galvez (1995), Theil and Fink (1983), and Theil and Deepak (1994). Others include Cambell and Katz (1975), Kates and Haarmann (1992), and Diamond (1997). Indeed, the empirical evidence is unequivocal and easily verified. Across numerous measures of income or consumption (adjusted or unadjusted for purchasing power parities), explained variances using either latitude, a nonlinear transformation of latitude, or temperature generally ranges between 50 to 70 percent. For example, Theil and Galvez (1995) find that some 67 percent of the cross-country variance in GDP per capita can be explained by absolute latitude; see also Williamson and Ross (1993).

This result is so pronounced that it appears even if the sample is limited to only the Northern Hemisphere, the Southern Hemisphere, or a given longitude, irrespective of the degree (e.g., the Europe-Africa axis, the Asia-Pacific axis, or the Americas).[4] For continents that span most climatic zones, the paradox also appears (e.g., North America, South America, Europe, Africa, Oceana, and Asia). Deviations from the pattern in the colder climates are easily identified as having restricted individual liberties or nonliberal economic policies (e.g., North Korea). Within the club of former communist countries the same pattern nevertheless emerges, with the equatorial countries having lower incomes and consumption (e.g., Benin), compared to the higher-latitude countries (e.g., Poland or Russia). Given the cross-sectional nature of the data, the shear magnitude of the explained variance is all the more surprising when comparing this naïve model to modern models of economic growth. The latter, when applied to the same data, reach these explained variances by relying on five to ten variables (many of which are also highly correlated with, or, perhaps, endogenous to latitude).

The paradox is not a static phenomenon. In a world where markets are globalizing and liberal economics is gradually replacing centralized planning, one might expect the effect of the paradox to attenuate as time progresses. The opposite is the case. Using a static sample of countries for which purchasing power parity adjustments are available (Summers and Heston 1991, 1993), one finds the explained variance of latitude has risen from approximately 40

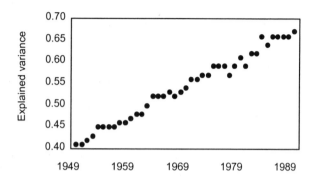

Figure 1.1
Latitude's explained variance of income: 1950−1990 (R^2 statistic, across static sample of sixty-six countries)

percent in 1950 to almost 70 percent by 1990.[5] As shown in figure 1.1, this progression has been both gradual and persistent. Not only does one need to explain why the paradox exists now and may persist in the future, but also why it has gradually increased in a regular fashion over time, probably starting sometime before the last century.

The Equatorial Paradox, across Cultures

Perhaps the most intriguing aspect of the paradox is that it is not limited to a specific form of aggregation: e.g., national versus transnational definitions. The observation that income varies across cultural groups often arises in discussions of economic history, the most famous observation coming from Max Weber (1920) who associated Protestantism, and in particular Calvinism, which culturally promoted modern-day capitalism, with a higher work ethic and higher levels of output per capita. A more recent follower of this idea includes Landes (1998) who associates many cultural factors to economic growth patterns, including the effect that religion plays on gender roles (p. 413):

> In general, the best clue to a nation's growth and development potential is the status and role of women. This is the greatest handicap of Muslim Middle Eastern societies today, the flaw that most bars them from modernity.

Treating a cultural group as a unit of observation proves difficult as many of the world religions are geographically dispersed across the planet. Protestants, for example, can be found in large numbers in 142 countries, Roman Catholics in 159, Muslims in 123, Jews in 113, Buddhists in 27, traditional beliefs (fetishism) in 89 and the Baha'i in 187 countries. Incorporating dummy variables for each religious group into a cross-sectional analysis also proves difficult given the large number of world religions (about 60). Similar problems arise when considering ethnic groups and linguistic groups which far out number countries. Treating each religion (language or ethnic group) as a transnational unit of observation (as opposed to a country), however, proves insightful to the paradox.

Table 1.1 reports income estimates across a sample of major religious groups that are aggregated across all countries. The data reported were created using the following methodology. All of the world's inhabitants were enumerated across 234 countries or territories. An in-depth classification was done on each population, broken down by religious belief, ethnic origin, and mother-tongue language. For example, the smallest entity considered was Pitcairn Island in the South Pacific; Pitcairn has 49 Euronesian inhabitants (descendants from the Bounty mutineers) who affirm being Seventh-day Adventists. A cultural group was deemed to be significant within a given locality if it showed up in national or international statistical sources. These classifications, across various sources, were combined into a unique breakdown for each country. Then, weighted averages across a number of variables, including income and latitude, were created for each cultural grouping across all localities. Although some estimation issues arise when using this approach, the magnitude of differences across the groups overwhelms possible measurement problems.[6]

At first glance, table 1.1 confirms the notion that culture may be associated with long-run growth as one finds substantial income variation across religious groups (the weighted average of current GNP per capita in 1994 US$). The religion with highest income is Protestant (Lutheran Evangelical) at $28,700, followed by Shinto at $26,900. Across all Protestant faiths, however, the average is $13,700, which is lower than Jews at $16,100 but above

Table 1.1
Income per capita across religions (1994 $US, GNP/capita)

Religious group	Income per capita	Latitude
Aglipayan	860	11
Traditional beliefs	644	14
Indigenous Christian	1,210	15
Afro-American Spiritists	2,620	16
Baha'i	2,080	16
Catholic Evangelical	2,680	16
Spiritist	2,840	17
Hindu	392	21
Jain	368	21
Sikh	702	22
Muslim, total	1,720	23
Buddhist	6,740	25
Roman Catholic	7,510	27
Muslim, Sunni	1,800	29
Muslim, Shia	3,910	31
Christian total	8,230	32
Chinese Folk	1,070	33
Atheist	3,190	35
Protestant, total	13,700	36
Shamanist	5,210	37
Shinto	26,900	37
Orthodox, Greek	7,180	39
Anglican	13,600	41
Jewish	16,100	41
Methodist	20,100	41
Presbyterian	20,900	41
Pentecostal	20,400	42
Church of God	22,000	43

Table 1.1 (continued)

Religious group	Income per capita	Latitude
Seventh Day Adventist	22,600	43
Baptist	22,700	44
Episcopalian	23,300	44
Jehovah's Witness	23,300	44
Mormon	22,900	44
Calvinist	10,100	47
Orthodox, Eastern	5,030	47
Reformed	21,300	47
Lutheran	20,200	49
Reformed Dutch	18,300	52
Lutheran-Evangelical	28,700	60

Notes: Adapted from Parker (1997a).

Roman Catholics at $7,510 and Muslims at $1,720. The low-income groups include the Jains at $368, the Hindus at $392, traditional beliefs at $644, and the Aglipayan at $860. A noticeable outlier is Eastern Orthodox which is heavily concentrated in former communist Europe.

The simple correlation between latitude and income is .81; 64 percent of the variance is explained by a linear equation, while 68 percent of the variance is explained by an exponential curve (log of income regressed against latitude); by removing the Eastern Orthodox religion, latitude explains 70 percent of the variance, closely in line with the result across countries.

Perhaps more exogenous to religion are the world's linguistic origins or cultures and, further still, the world's ethnic groups. Using the same methodology as described earlier, economic development indicators were estimated for the world's linguistic and ethnic cultures.[7]

Table 1.2 shows the dispersion of income across the world's most populous language groups (selected from over 400 aggregated language groups).

The highest income language group across those listed is Japanese at $26,900, followed by German at $22,300. Mother-tongue speakers of Bengali and Marathi have the lowest levels of income at $275 and $369, respectively.

Similar to religions, one observes extremely wide dispersions of incomes per capita being explained by latitude with the simple correlation being high and statistically significant (.69, *p-value* < .0001). Similar to religions, both linear and exponential models fit the data well (R^2 = .48, and .57 respectively). Again, by eliminating the languages heavily dominated by former communist regimes (i.e., Chinese and Russian), the R^2 statistic increases to .60 and .61, respectively, and the coefficient on latitude is highly significant (*p-value* < .0001).

Parker (1997c) provides similar data across the world's 400-plus major ethnic groups. Using this form of aggregation, the dispersion is at its highest. Norwegian, Romansch, Swiss, Liechtensteiner, Luxemburger, Japanese, Finnish,

Table 1.2

Income per capita across languages (1994 $US, GNP/capita)

Language group	Income per capita	Latitude
Javanese	693	5
Vietnamese	442	16
Portuguese	3,230	18
Tamil	425	20
Hindi	376	21
Marathi	369	21
Telugu	370	21
Bengali	275	23
Spanish	5,260	23
Urdu	394	23
Punjabi	413	27
Arabic	2,400	28
Chinese	611	34
Japanese	26,900	37
Korean	5,030	37
Turkish	4,240	39
Italian	18,700	42
English	21,200	45
French	20,700	47
German	22,300	50
Russian	5,650	54

Notes: Adapted from Parker (1997a).

Swedish, Danish, and Icelander top the list as the highest income ethnic groups, all exceeding $23,600 GNP per capita. At the lowest levels of income are the Malawi, Makua, Saho, Tsonga, Tigre, Tigrinya, Amhara, Oromo, Gurage, Ometo and Sidamo, all of which have GNP per capitas less than $130. The ethnographer will note that the low-income ethnic groups are generally of the black race, whereas the high income ethnic groups are not. As with religious and language groups, one finds a statistically significant relationship across the full sample with similar levels of explained variance (i.e., some 60 percent for linear and nonlinear models). Ethnicity being exogenous to both language and religion, it may be tempting to leap to the conclusion that long-run climatically driven genetic or racial differences determine long-run income dispersion. Careful study, however, reveals that this is not the case. The lack of careful reflection, in fact, has lead to a proliferation of less than satisfactory explanations of this paradox.

Explanations

Researchers have generally approached the equatorial paradox in three ways. The first is to ignore it, as noted earlier by Streeten (1971, p. 78):

> Perhaps the most striking fact is that most underdeveloped countries lie in the tropical and semi-tropical zones, between the Tropic of Cancer and the Tropic of Capricorn. Recent writers have too easily glossed over this fact and considered it largely fortuitous. This reveals a deep-seated optimistic bias with which we approach problems of development and the reluctance to admit the vast differences in initial conditions with which

today's poor countries are faced compared with the pre-industrial phase of more advanced countries.

Citing certain exceptions, others reject serious study of the phenomenon claiming that the relationship is spurious. The city-states of Singapore and Hong Kong are often cited. While these exceptions certainly do not explain the paradox, they are hardly useful in dispelling it outright. First, it is not obvious that if these cities were somehow averaged into their local regions (as most countries consist of both rural and urban areas), that these exceptions would appear so striking. More important, it becomes difficult to isolate the effects of location from economic performance for these examples. Regnier in his study of Singaporean economic growth notes (1991, p. 2):

> A glance at the map of South-East Asia makes it clear how great is the geostrategic importance of the Strait of Malacca linking the Indian Ocean and the South China Sea, which would confer great maritime and commercial power on any form of state organization capable of controlling this pivotal zone. At least since the second century AD, this attribute has caused a series of state organizations, definable as maritime commercial emporia, to emerge and then disappear in the vicinity of the Strait. Singapore is only the latest in this series.

In a second study, Huff (1994, p. 1) also notes that this locational advantage is not recent:

> Economic development in Singapore is not new. Rapid late nineteenth century growth had produced a large, modern city on the island by 1900. In 1939, and even more in 1959, when British colonial rule effectively ended, Singapore was a metropolis. . . . During the 1950s Singapore already had higher per capita income than almost anywhere else in Asia.

Huff concludes (p. 7) that "the basis for the economic development of Singapore was — and for most of its history has remained — geography." Stamford Raffles (1830, p. 378) wrote that his decision to choose Singapore island as an entrepot was to combine "every possible advantage, geographical and local." Granted, geography alone did not create Singapore and Hong Kong. Smart policies (or the avoidance of bad ones) had much to do with where these cities are today. Without location advantages, however, it is not clear that these policies would have resulted in similar economic growth had the peoples of these cities been living inland, 500 kilometers away.

The second general approach is to implicitly accept cross-latitude differences and control for these in an econometric fashion. This is typically achieved by using regional dummy variables or some other proxies. The shortcoming of this approach is that it provides no theoretical explanation for the phenomenon. It is also difficult to interpret significant coefficients (vis-à-vis theory or policy). The categorical variables themselves may proxy for critical, yet unidentified, factors affecting growth.

The third approach is to provide other explanations for the phenomenon, though these have proven to be far from compelling. Commonly cited factors include the existence of work-inhibiting diseases that are bound to tropical zones. African trypanosomiasis or sleeping sickness, for example, exists only within a range of 10 degrees north or south of the equator.[8] Agriculture in the tropics is also subject to specific pests, periodic draughts, and soil depletion. Vectors that can affect human health (e.g., malaria) and agricultural production are also common in the tropics (Karamarck 1967). It is further argued that the tropics have been geographically at a disadvantage vis-à-vis trade routes that might have allowed for faster diffusion of productivity-enhancing technologies (see Diamond 1997).

A less benevolent explanation for why tropical regions have low income is the lack of a work ethic; it is simply too hot to work. Conversely, cold climates invigorate workers.[9] Others claim that little work is needed to survive given the proximity of food that can be "easily picked from the local bushes." Others have used racial explanations (e.g., Huntington 1912). More recently, Hall and Jones (1999, p. 112) find that "the bulk of the simple correlation between distance from the equator and economic performance occurs because historical circumstances lead this variable to proxy well for social infrastructure." They define social infrastructure as a composite index covering law and order, bureaucratic quality, corruption, risk of expropriation, government repudiation of contracts, and the extent to which a country is open to international trade. For some unidentified historical or theoretical reasons, the tropics are believed to have somehow bred corruption. Others consider geographic disposition, but abstract away from the issue of latitude. Krugman and Venables (1995), for example, consider a "north" and "south," and they focus on trade and transportation costs. These and similar works model geographic disparities with latitude-implied labels, though the results might be derived by any two separate economies (not necessarily across latitudes).

Rebuttals

These and similar explanations of the equatorial grand canyon are generally discarded as lacking theoretical and empirical rigor. They fail to indicate the extent to which things would be different if these dependencies were somehow removed (i.e., diseases were eradicated, education or social infrastructure were equalized across all latitudes, etc.). Furthermore, some tropical countries have overcome these problems and have enjoyed high life expectancies and literacy but remain in the low-income bracket (with the exception of off-shore banking and holiday centers like the Cayman Islands). The equatorial phenomenon has also persisted in spite of substantial development efforts. The "Pacific paradox," for example, has been a long-debated regional and international subject. Why is it that most Pacific Island countries have slow per-capita growth rates despite having substantial foreign aid, high levels of education, and favorable natural resource endowments?[10]

Similarly, a number of wealthy countries whose territories extend across a large range of latitudes are subject to the paradox despite having the same rule of law, low levels of corruption, identical educational institutions, high-quality health care (low infant mortalities and high life expectancies), and access to liberal economic markets. For many of these countries, where the territories have been within the same sovereign state for over 50 to 200 years, the latitude effect is often more pronounced compared to the sample of the world's nations.

The 1998 *CIA World Factbook* reports high-income countries with overseas processions and their incomes per capita. Those having equatorial territories include France, Britain, New Zealand, and the United States. In addition to its European presence, France, for example, also encompasses Mayotte, Wallis and Futuna, Martinique, French Polynesia, Guadeloupe, New Caledonia, and Reunion. Similar lists exist for the other countries. Across these four cases, the paradox reappears; the probability, in all cases, that this has occurred from chance is less than .0001. Eliminating places that serve as military installations, research outposts and lighthouses, or similarly subsidized economies (e.g.,

Guam), the explained variances revealed for France is 53 percent, 89 percent for New Zealand, 76 percent for the United States (56 percent including Guam), and 77 percent for the United Kingdom.[11] Combined, some 70 percent of income dispersion in these developed countries is explained by latitude. In spite of these countries sharing broadly the same economic policy (e.g., monetary policy), legal structure (intellectual property and trade practices), social infrastructure, and access to business institutions, the paradox persists.

For some countries or integrated trading regions that have contiguous territories spanning multiple latitudes, a similar pattern emerges, though it is generally less pronounced since few countries cover radically different regions. Italy, of course, is notorious for the paradox. Latitude explains some 85 percent of the variance of income across its regions, excluding the capital city (75 percent when Rome is included).[12] The historical existence of similar patterns in Brazil, China, India, Russia, and the continental United States, though more limited in latitudes than global variances, makes the paradox all the more puzzling. In other words, the phenomenon may not be a purely "cross-country" issue.

A Tropical Bias

An understanding why tropical countries might have lower steady-state incomes can at best only capture part of the paradox. Income gradually rises as one gets farther from the equator. It is a fallacy to think that the distribution is bimodal with only two types of development: rich-cold and poor-hot countries. The paradox also lies in the fact that there appears to be a continuum. Mediterranean countries are generally more wealthy than equatorial countries, and temperate countries are generally more wealthy than Mediterranean countries, and Nordic countries tend to be more wealthy than temperate countries. This is especially problematic given that all of these countries started a few hundred years ago in low-income positions facing equally daunting growth barriers or path dependencies when judged by today's standards. Indeed, the paradox can be framed as seeking to understand what drove the colder regions of the world to increase their consumption levels and technology beyond those in Mediterranean regions. Why do Mediterranean regions have higher incomes than subtropical regions? Why are consumption levels higher in the subtropics compared to the equatorial topics? The paradox is further complicated by the fact that one observes similar variations in cultures that have never industrialized in both cold and hot regions (e.g., comparing the production and consumption behaviors of hunter-gatherers across the arctic tundra with those of the equator).[13]

Well before modern dispersions of income per capita, certain scholars foresaw such variances. Their thoughts were squarely placed on the direct effects of the variable in question—the inclination of the sun to the horizon and the resulting climatology. Though different climates can exist at the same latitude (due to other physical dispositions), latitude drives the world's climatic variations. Indeed, trying to explain the equatorial paradox while ignoring solar radiation, or *heat transfer*, may be as difficult as explaining monetary inflation while ignoring the money supply. Anyone having studied thermodynamics knows that *heat transfer* is both a precise and particularly complex concept that cannot be treated without considering broader issues (e.g., the system definition). Earlier thinkers tended to consider this issue by mostly using classic and renaissance intuition of physics and physiology.

Notions of Physical Explanations

As early as 400 B.C., Hippocrates, in *Air, Waters and Places*, noted that climate generally drives basic physiological wants and needs, psychological well-being, and health care in general. The effect was felt to be so pronounced as to drive cultural traits (mores). Similar thoughts were espoused by the fourteenth-century Arab philosopher and historian Ibn Khaldun, in *The Muquaddimah: An Introduction to History*, who considered climate an important driver of world history to that point.

Among the early believers that heat transfer, or similar concepts, might have a persistent influence, Montesquieu (1748) can not be overlooked. A politician-vintner from Bordeaux, Montesquieu was widely read in his time, belonged to the Encyclopedists of the French Enlightenment, and was a contemporary colleague to Denis

Diderot, Jean Jacques Rousseau, Baron von Grimm, Friedrich Melchior, and Voltaire. In his later years, Montesquieu corresponded with David Hume whose pupil, Adam Smith, is known to have read and been influenced by his works. Montesquieu's claim to fame in the Anglo-Saxon world, at least, is his idea that central governments should consist of three independent branches that provide checks and balances.

His most influential work is *The Spirit of the Laws* which comprises thirty-one books spanning politics, economics, and sociology. *The Laws,* to Montesquieu, were none other than certain laws of nature (physics and physiology) that at the time were ill-defined but within reach of intuition. Based on this and his other works, encyclopedias of today write of Montesquieu's collective thoughts as "the precursor of many branches of modern social sciences . . . by showing the interrelation of economical, geographical, political, religious, and social forces in history."[14]

Using rather crude biological experiments such as examining skin temperature and blood circulation in farm animals (mostly sheep), Montesquieu may have been the first to discover a link between economics and physics-based physiology. Lacking precise terms for neurotransmitters or hormones, Montesquieu explained cross-country differences in consumption and income by claiming that "juices" flowing in the body motivated humans to achieve certain steady-state behaviors, or what today is known in physiology as homeostatic equilibrium.

From there, he made cross-country comparisons of utility and also global forecasts of the consumption/production of alcohol, clothing, housing, food, industrial machinery, suicide, war, and sex. Unlike Smith, who commented mostly on nations within the same latitudes (Europe and North America), Montesquieu focused on variations across latitudes (comparing northern and southern regions of Europe, Africa, Asia, and the Americas).

Montesquieu's eclectic and multidisciplinary approach correctly predicted the higher levels of economic development of temperate countries (e.g., northern Europe) than warmer countries (southern Europe), versus hotter countries (India and in Africa). While the colder countries would amass material wealth and higher levels of consumption, he foresaw these countries having higher suicide rates from their psychological misery. The sheer variety and accuracy of his forecasts, shown later, are all the more remarkable given the timing of his writing. As we will see later, in 1748 there was low variance in real incomes per capita across the world, as the industrial revolution had yet to start in earnest (1760−1770). Furthermore, no reliable data sources existed for cross-country comparisons.

Montesquieu was armed with an intuition for thermodynamics and neurophysiology, and the sources of his data were correspondents from all over the world (Japan, China, India, the Americas, Africa), across a number of disciplines (mostly his Encyclopedist friends).

The key breakthrough made by Montesquieu is the thought that income is not generated for income's sake. Rather, income is generated by humans who are driven to consume (today and in anticipation of the future). Consumption, in turn, is driven by psychological needs (utility). These psychological motivations are driven by physiological mechanisms (the brain), which adhere to certain laws of nature (physics — thermodynamics). If the implications of fundamental physics vary from place to place, so too should the effects on physiology, psychology, utility, steady-state consumption motivation, and income. Countries can, therefore, have different levels of income but attain similar levels of physiological and psychological comfort or satisfaction. In economic parlance, marginal utilities can approach zero in different countries, or equalize across different cultural groups, at different levels of consumption.

Perhaps the most important strength of Montesquieu was his ability to recognize social structures, policies, or institutions as being logically endogenous to basic physical principles. The following passage, one of many in the same vein, is classic Montesquieu in this regard (1748, p. 239):

> The law of Mohammed that prohibits the drinking of wine is, therefore, a law of the climate of Arabia; thus, before Mohammed, water was the ordinary drink of the Arabs. The law that prohibits the Carthaginians from drinking wine was also a law of the climate; in effect, the climate of these two

countries is about the same. Such a law would not be good in cold climates, where the climate seems to force a certain drunkenness of the nation quite different from drunkenness of the person. Drunkenness is found established around the world in proportion to the cold and dampness of the climate. As you go from the equator to our pole, you will see drunkenness increase with the degree of latitude. As you go from the same equator to the opposite pole, you will find drunkenness to the south, as on our side to the north. . . . A German drinks by custom, a Spaniard by choice.

In line with a number of economic policies discussed later in chapter 7, had Americans correctly interpreted Montesquieu's insight, they might have avoided the calamity of prohibition. To Montesquieu, something more fundamental than Al Capone drove America to overturn the eighteenth amendment's prohibition on alcohol.

Montesquieu's Mechanism: A Preview

Lacking the benefits of modern science, Montesquieu never fully comprehended the laws of energy conservation or the physiological mechanisms that might simultaneously be responsible for such unrelated variables as cross-country suicide rates and economic behavior. The primary neurophysiological mechanism that must adhere to *the laws* may turn out to be the single most important determinant of long-run economic variances across countries. That neurological mechanism is the hypothalamus. To present-day neurophysiologists, the pea-sized hypothalamus located in the forebrain is now considered "the brain's interface with the hormonal and autonomic systems that controls the body's internal homeostasis"(Carpenter 1996, p. 7). To students of biological psychology, it is seen as affecting "one or more motivated behaviors, such as feeding, drinking, temperature regulation, sexual behavior, fighting, or activity level"(Kalat 1998, p. 87). Medical students are told that it is responsible for the 4 F's: "feeding, fleeing, fighting, and mating." Students of economics are told little.[15] What they miss is the fact that the hypothalamus is the linchpin behind utility functions — it is the boundary maker for rational decisions — the source of aggregate preferences. A causal model of utility, if it were to be developed, must include a discussion of the hypothalamus as *the* key biological mechanism allowing us to adhere to the laws of physics.

Though many brain and body functions are critically important, what makes the hypothalamus of interest is its role as a "Grand Central Station." The hypothalamus acts as an interface between the blood stream and the brain while linking external stimuli (the five senses of smell, sight, touch, taste, and sound) and external responses (including economic behavior) to internal stimuli and internal responses. It drives motivation, monitors homeostasis, and ultimately keeps us alive via neural, autonomic, and hormonal adjustments. While other regions of the brain allow for sophisticated sensory analysis and motor coordination, Carpenter (1996, p. 278) notes (in reference to all neural mechanisms):

> But in the end, the only part that really matters is the region where the four fundamental kinds of inputs and outputs actually come together. That region is the hypothalamus: though scarcely larger than a peanut, it determines all we do.

The Objective

A careful examination of Montesquieu's logic follows here and it is updated for the 250 years that have since transpired. In doing so, one may begin to answer long-standing questions. What will be the likely patterns of long-run economic growth as the aforementioned path dependencies (starting conditions), or barriers to growth, are gradually identified and removed? If countries do not converge to the same absolute level of consumption or income, what will be the magnitude of differences? Under a divergence scenario, is it possible that marginal utilities or certain qualities of life can converge? Models from physics and physiology not only help answer these questions, but they also suggest the functional forms of basic relationships (e.g., that certain consumption functions are kinked). The primary artifact resulting from this line of query, however, is insight into optimal political strategies that would not be otherwise observable. One can show, as

Fogel suggested, that these concepts can be reconciled with existing growth frameworks.

The Basic Argument

The basic logic is similar to that used by Montesquieu. The form and level of economic growth will largely be in line with rational utility maximization, provided this is allowed by central authorities. For reasons relating to thermal physics and physiology, utility functions are, and will remain, divergent across countries. The drive to maximize utility (largely a neurophysiological process) will lead to different steady-state growth dynamics across various measures of economic behavior, both in the aggregate (the level of development) and the dissaggregate (the form of development). Countries with similar utility functions will converge to similar steady-states of growth and contemporaneous levels of development (many have already). This will arise irrespective of various inherent and frequently cited path dependencies. A full-information fully liberalized global economy with mobile human and physical capital will accelerate this divergence along conditional paths. For countries with similar political systems, institutions, and natural resources, those closer to the equator will be able to achieve similar marginal utilities at different levels of consumption to those located further toward the poles.

Summary

Coupled with factors that have received substantial attention elsewhere, evidence will be presented in support of the notion that long-run growth, and in particular, the observance of *conditional convergence*, can be causally attributed to variances in the working of the brain and, in particular, hypothalmic activity. Most extant econometric models of long-run economic growth can explain from 50 to 70 percent of the worldwide variances in income per capita. If even half of the remaining unexplained variances could be explained by physiological mechanisms, it may prove worthwhile to know what these mechanisms are and how they affect growth prospects.

A related implication is that a sufficiently large variance is explained by physiological differences in utility so as to taint current measures of income as proxies for economic well-being or performance (i.e., to levels beyond those already accounted for in adjustments for imperfections in exchange rates, or purchasing power parities). With objective and invariant measures of the "conditions" behind conditional convergence, one can create alternative measures of poverty and economic performance across countries. Just as one filters times series for seasonalities before drawing policy conclusions, so too must one filter consumption and income data across countries.

Data filtered for physical principles suggest that a country with a high level of income, for example, may be "poorer" and have lower economic performance than a country with lower income per capita. What today one sees as failures in economic development may, with the adjusted measures proposed, be considered growth successes. Countries that are "poor" (low performers) will grow faster than those that are "rich" (high performers). Many low performers can be, and have been, countries with high levels of income (e.g., the United States or the United Kingdom). High performers can include countries with relatively low incomes (e.g., Costa Rica, or, within Europe, Italy). Using these measures, the neoclassical predictions of Solow (1956) and, more recently, Barro (1997), among others, are confirmed.

The book concludes with comments on the implied effects on economic policy. One finding concurs with the generally held view that "fine tuning" does not alter steady state paths, as noted by Barro and Sala-i-Martin (1995, p. 4−5):

> ... if we can learn about government policy options that have even small effects on the long-term growth rate, then we can contribute much more to improvements in standards of living than has been provided by the entire history of macroeconomic analysis of countercyclical policy and fine tuning. Economic growth ... is the part of macroeconomics that really matters.

This book goes beyond this, however, by also finding that physics prevents universally applicable or absolute standards of living that can be used as benchmarks for all peoples of the world. Physiology may ultimately be the part of economic growth that matters. Whether living in Sweden or Indonesia, we are studying the behavior of a genetically evolved primate mammal and this fact matters.

Notes

1. This view should not to be confused with that of the physiocrats of France who drew analogies between the human body and macroeconomics. *Physioeconomics* is the economics of physics-based physiology, as affected by physiography (climate and terrain).

2. *Principles of Economics*, I, p. 59.

3. See also Cigno (1981), Krugman (1991) and Stiglitz (1974).

4. Data supplied in Parker (1997d) cover 400 climatic and related economic variables upon which the conclusions of this paragraph are based.

5. Source data are reported in Summers and Heston (1993), the Penn World Tables, version 5.5.

6. A more detailed discussion of the methodology and caveats are presented in Parker (1997a).

7. Parker (1997b) and (1997c) report over 400 variables for each.

8. James C. McKinley, Jr., "Sleeping Sickness Rakes War-Torn Sudan," *International Herald Tribune*, July 19 − 20, 1997, p. 2.

9. A curious note relating temperature and work effort is offered in Barro (1989, p. 999) who writes "if it gets really hot, people work a lot and pay little attention to the wage."

10. Gordon Bilney, "The Pacific Island States, Rich in Resources, Need to do Better," *International Herald Tribune*, August 1, 1994, p. 4.

11. Figures for France exclude French Guyana and St. Pierre et Miquelon; figures for the United Kingdom exclude Cayman Islands and Bermuda. Inclusion of these reduce explained variances, though latitude remains significant at p-$value$<.0001. All R^2 figures in this and the next paragraph are from a univariate exponential model regressing latitude with income per capita (latest figures, adjusting for purchasing power parity). Linear models show a similar fit.

12. Using data reported from the European Union, reported in the *Financial Times*, April 23, 1998, p. IV.

13. Though arctic hunter-gathers have almost vanished, the Nenets, who number approximately 1,000 of the arctic Siberian coast, eat raw fish, drink reindeer blood, and live year-round in reindeer-skin tepees called chums. Every year they migrate some 1,000 miles with their herds across the tundra; as reported by Michael Specter, "Arctic Tribe in Russia May be Key to Migration Mystery," *International Herald Tribune*, November 24, 1994, p. 9.

14. From the 1997 electronic encyclopedia, *Encarta*; Microsoft Corporation.

15. See Morgane and Panksepp (1980) *Behavioral Studies of the Hypothalamus*, and the earlier volumes, *Anatomy of the Hypothalamus and Physiology of the Hypothalamus*, for a complete review.

...without the data, yo' chatta don't matta.

— Tony Rothman, paraphrasing Johannes Kepler[1]

Empirical regularities make growth one of the more intriguing topics in economics. The previous chapter highlighted three such regularities: (1) incomes per capita systematically increase with absolute latitude — often called the equatorial paradox; latitude explains from 50 to 70 percent of worldwide variances in income; the paradox also appears in highly developed countries with equatorial territories or regions; (2) the correlation between latitude and income is gradually increasing over time; and (3) the equatorial paradox is not a bimodal canyon, but more of a deep valley; income gradually increases as one crosses latitudes. The paradox is replicated across geographies (e.g., by longitude, hemisphere, or continent), definitions of observational units, or levels of aggregation, provided these span many latitudes, including countries, contiguous trading areas, cultures, political blocs, or currency unions.[2]

Table 2.1 shows the population sizes, incomes, latitudes, and average prevailing temperatures for a variety of countries. They were selected to contrast the sensitivity of these variables to country size, level of consumption, and previous affiliation to communism. Notwithstanding very few and sparsely populated exceptions, the paradox holds for those countries which make up over 99.8 percent of the world's population. While one might view the outliers themselves as paradoxical, they too demand explanation.

In addition to these three regularities, I will briefly highlight others that become important in framing the notion that physiology might be related to growth. These are (4) conditional convergence in income is a long-run process, (5) conditional convergence is measurement sensitive, leading to two popular growth fallacies, and (6) economic data are becoming more spatially correlated over time, although the spatial correlation is not symmetric. To these we can also add those previously noted in Kaldor (1961), Lucas (1988), Romer (1989), and Jones (1998), who note that growth rates have been linked to growth in trade, and that historical migration has been from poor countries to rich countries; stylized facts the book will return to in chapter 8.[3]

Table 2.1
Climate across countries

Country	Population 1994, m	Income	Temp. in °C	Degrees latitude
Noncommunist populous				
Germany	81	20,800	8	51
USA	258	30,200	12	44
Japan	125	24,500	15	37
Mexico	90	7,700	16	24
Pakistan	128	2,600	22	29
India	897	1,600	24	21
Brazil	156	6,300	25	16
Bangladesh	122	1,330	25	23
Indonesia	195	4,600	28	5
Nigeria	107	1,300	28	9
Highest-lowest consumption				
Norway	4	27,400	5	64
Switzerland	7	23,800	9	47
Mozambique	16	800	27	23
Somalia	10	600	28	5
Communist—former				
Russia	149	4,700	3	55
China	1210	3,460	11	35
Vietnam	70	1,700	25	15
Cuba	11	1,540	25	22
Benin	5	1,900	27	6
"Outliers"				
Bermuda	0.062	29,000	22	32
Kuwait	2	22,300	25	29
Cayman Islands	0.031	23,800	26	19
Brunei	0.3	18,000	27	5

Regularity 4: Conditional Convergence Is a Long-Run Process

Definitions

Modern models of growth have yielded two useful concepts of convergence (see, for example, Barro and Sala-i-Martin 1995, pp. 383−387). Convergence may be observed as a trend toward an absolute level of income, whereby low-income countries grow faster than high-income countries (β convergence), or an absolute convergence in dispersion (σ convergence). In the latter case, countries converge to a steady-state level of variance; the direction from which they do so can be evaluated by long-run trends (e.g., measured variances in the logarithms of income or some similar measures).

These forms of convergence are traditionally investigated using a functional form similar to the one given in equation 2.1 (from Evans and Karras 1993, p. 150). If c_{it} is the logarithm of consumption per capita in country i (i = 1, 2, ..., I) at time t (increasing annually from t_0 to T), g_i is the average growth rate in consumption, or $g_i = (c_{iT} - c_{i0})/(T-t_0)$,

$$g_i = \alpha + \beta c_{i0} + \gamma' x_i + \varepsilon_i \tag{2.1}$$

Tests of convergence mostly rely on estimates of β and γ. If γ is imposed to equal zero and β is significantly negative, then the data reveal an absolute convergence across countries; low consumption countries grow faster than high consumption countries. If β is negative and certain variables applied to γ are statistically significant, then one observes conditional convergence. Countries tend to converge to similar steady states conditioned on the variables in x_i (e.g., political institutions, natural resources, etc.). Countries having similar values in x_i form *convergence clubs*. If β is positive or statistically insignificant, then consumption levels diverge.

Early growth research made an implicit assumption that convergence was absolute in nature (e.g., Baumol 1986). A healthy debate has occurred since over estimation procedures and, more fundamentally, the correct x_i's to include in functions like equation 2.1.[4] Time frames, measures of income or consumption, x_i's and sample sizes have varied across studies that collectively demonstrate the conditional convergence phenomenon.[5]

In a purely descriptive manner, one can gain insight into convergence dynamics using figure 2.1, adapted from Barro and Sala-i-Martin (1995, p. 385). If one observes cross-country variances in measured development (e.g., logarithms of income) falling from a given time origin, one infers that variances started above their steady state. If variances increase over time, one concludes that they started below their steady state. If variances remain constant over time, then they started in their steady states. The steady state, barring any major shocks across countries, may be readily observed from cross-sectional time series covering a sufficiently long duration.

Minimally, one needs to establish some fixed origin in time, t_0, from which to begin measuring variances. Establishing a time origin is a critical issue in growth economics. The time origin can have dramatic effects on both the choice of x_i's and the completeness of the theoretical explanation. Choosing t_0 too close to the current date may lead to selecting x_i's, or initial conditions of heterogeneity that themselves are endogenous to other factors. The observer is left to wonder how the countries became so heterogeneous in the first place (e.g., where did the initial levels of human capital come from?).

It will be shown that greatest "completeness" can only be offered by models explaining contemporaneous dispersions of *absolute* consumption or income per capita; models considering growth *rates*, say, calculated since the 1950s or 1960s are less complete. It so happens that absolute consumption and income levels today perfectly reflect each countries' *long-run* growth rates, if one is careful about choosing the time origin.

Time Origins of Growth

The separation of human history into phases will always suffer from the ad hoc nature of the cutoffs, however, the choice of the starting point should not be arbitrary. Sometime prior to the industrial revolution, which most

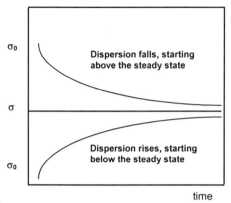

Figure 2.1
Dispersion and steady states (adapted from Barro and Sala-i-Martin, p. 385)

historians place as starting in England sometime in the mid- to late-eighteenth century, incomes around the world were at a low, if not subsistence, level. Historical records, as they stand today, reveal substantial divergences thereafter.

Kuznets (1966) argued that true economic divergence did not occur until sometime after 1500. While a lot of human economic history came before then, for the common man precarious subsistence had remained the basic concern. Wealth, where it was generated prior to 1500, remained in the hands of a small elite (mostly land or slave owners, traders, bureaucrats, and clergy). Not until the 1500s did wealth trickle to the masses in such a way that all could benefit, excluding slaves. This period saw the emergence of "protocapitalism." For the first time, marked yet sustained differences in the level of economic development across peoples around the world were observed, especially coinciding with the emergence of European technology (Landes 1998).

Most now accept that there was a general kink in the world's growth curves some time around the French revolution. From that point on, sustained variances in economic growth were observed across countries, traces of which can be seen in today's figures of income per capita. Maddison (1995, p. 31), in developing historical estimates, argues that the protocapitalist period ended in the early nineteenth century:

> Simon Kuznets (1966) put the turning point for "modern economic growth" at 1750, but in light of recent evidence suggesting that growth in the eighteenth century was slower than previously thought (Crafts, 1985), I prefer to use 1820 as a starting point. Recent evidence has also falsified the earlier view, espoused most strongly by Rostow (1960) and Gerschenkron (1962), that there was a long drawn-out sequence of staggered "takeoffs" in West European countries throughout the nineteenth century. It now seems clear that growth was generally much faster after 1820 than it was in the "protocapitalist" period from 1500 to 1820, when Western Europe was slowly pulling ahead of the rest of the world.

Several reasons can be advanced supporting the idea that growth should be analyzed over a time frame starting some 250 to 500 years ago. Most important, much of the dynamics of conditional convergence observed today finds its origins in variances beginning well before the 1960s (a typical starting point for empirical studies of growth). If complete explanation is desired, one must select an origin well before then.

A number of authors have taken on the challenge of compiling historical series covering the last 200 years across a rather impressive sample of countries. Although the reliability of data covering the period prior to 1900 might be questioned, even if the sources of these are off by several orders of magnitude in any single year or longer epoch, the dynamics of present-day divergence swamp these potential measurement errors.

Figure 2.2 plots GDP per capita for 57 countries from 1820 to 1992 (in 1990 international dollars) as estimated by Maddison (1995); his sample covers over 90 percent of the world's total population and consumption, and spans all continents and latitudes. Figure 2.3 summarizes the dynamics of both means (μ) and standard deviations (σ) across this sample of latitudes. Standard deviations and means are plotted on the same graph so that both are directly interpretable (log transformations yield the same results). Identical inferences can be drawn from the historical series offered by Bairoch (1981) who estimated the growth dynamics of GNP per capita for the period 1830

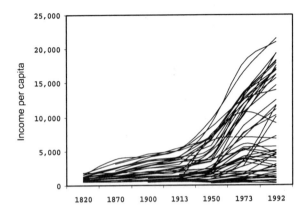

Figure 2.2
GDP per capita (1990 international dollars) in fifty-six countries
(Maddison 1995)

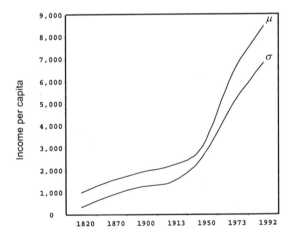

Figure 2.3
Mean and dispersion of GDP per capita across fifty-six countries:
1820–1992 (Maddison 1995)

to 1970 across a sample of seventeen mostly OECD and European Union countries.[6]

Absolute Income and the Growth Rate

Using percentages suggested in Maddison (p. 19) one can back extrapolate from his sample of countries using 0.2 percent growth for Western Europe, 0.1 percent for the rest of Europe and Latin America, and 0.0 percent for Asia and Africa. It turns out that the sample of economies studied were convergent in the year 1463, which in the grand scheme of things comes very close to the year 1500 proposed by Kuznets. The extrapolated level of income per capita in 1463 was $572, very close to the $565 estimate for the average worldwide income per capita in the year 1500 given by Maddison (using 1990 international prices, p. 19). This level of income would reflect a subsistence farming economy with enough surplus to carry a central governing bureaucracy living in some degree of luxury. Based on more contemporaneous estimates of income per capita, countries studied by Maddison falling in or below the range of $500 to $600 over the past 30 years include Bangladesh, Burma, Ethiopia, Tanzania—countries that reasonably fit the description of agrarian subsistence economies having a central elite. The consistency of these numbers and the supporting historical record, then, places the world in a relatively convergent state of income per capita at the dawn of the European renaissance—a stylized fact one can use to calculate long-run growth rates.

Though longer time frames are surely preferable to shorter ones, one is left with the problem that many countries of importance in today's development efforts did not exist as units of observation prior to the 1960s, especially in Africa. It is mostly for this reason that many empirical studies of growth consider time frames starting in the 1960s. This problem is mitigated by the fact that incomes were largely convergent sometime before the fifteenth century.[7] For any location i in time t, the absolute growth of income or consumption, c_{it}, is $\Delta c_{it} = c_{it} - c_{i0}$. Since all countries began at the same absolute level as indicated above (e.g., \$572) in the fifteenth century, one can monotonically transform the series by subtracting that value from all observations at all moments in time; $c_{i0} = 0$ everywhere. Current levels of income per capita equivalently measure, therefore, the long-run growth rate; the two are perfectly correlated.

One can therefore study economic growth using a broad sample of countries, including those newly independent since the 1960s, provided that one understands that absolute consumption or income per capita variances observed across countries today reflect variances in the growth rate beginning sometime after the fifteenth century. In fact, if one started from the period studied by Maddison, the correlation between the growth rate since 1820, and the absolute levels of income per capita in 1992 is found to be extremely high (.86, *p-value*<.0001). Again, as figure 2.3 indicates, this is due to all series being relatively convergent in 1820, or some fifty years after the industrial revolution began in Britain. From that point on, growth rates appear to change to a far greater extent than over the previous 250-year period. This point is useful in comparing studies that use different time frames to test theories, but end with regressions explaining variances in current incomes per capita. In this way, they all study long-run growth rates from sometime around 1500, but mostly from the start of the industrial revolution sometime after 1750, as proposed by Kuznets.

When setting the time origin in this way, equation 2.1 is only affected by the selection of the x_i's; β disappears since c_{i0} has no variance across i.[8] Ideally, the x_i's used should have prevailed at the time origin and been heterogeneous across countries. Other variables meeting this criteria include religion and language. The application of latitude to equation 2.1 yields a significant γ (*p-value*<.0001) and explains almost 70 percent of cross-country variance in long-run growth rates.

Factors that were largely convergent at the time origin are problematic or may only provide incomplete long-run explanations. For these, one is left to explain why they might have changed over time. If drivers of these factors can be identified, one might best be served by directly applying these in equation 2.1. For example, initial levels of adult literacy might not meet the completeness criteria as these probably showed minimal global variance with mean values close to zero (though the Arab world might have been more developed on average for these measures at the time); similarly for human capital, or various measures of social infrastructure. Europe, for example, was frequently victim to the pest; urban and rural squalor was almost unimaginable by today's standards, even in comparison to present-day Africa, India, or Indonesia. The fifteenth century Gutenberg printing press had just been invented and literacy-based knowledge was mostly accessible to accountants, clergy, and a small aristocracy across most countries (e.g., from India to Scandinavia).

The remainder of the discussion will largely focus on explaining current variances in consumption or income per capita as our measure of economic growth, understanding that one is considering roughly a 250- to 500-year young process, as aptly characterized by Jones (1998, pp. 80–81):

> ... suppose we were to map out world history on a football field. Let the goal line on one end of the field stand for 1 million B.C., which is a conservative estimate of when humans first became distinguishable from other primates. Let the other goal line correspond to 2000 A.D. Humans were essentially hunters and gatherers for the overwhelming majority of history, until the development of agriculture approximately 10,000 years ago. On our football field, hunting and gathering occupies the first 99 yards of the 100 yard field; systematic agriculture begins on the one-yard line. The year 1 A.D. is only 7 inches from the goal line, and the Industrial Revolution begins less than one inch from the goal line. In the history of

humankind, the era of modern economic growth is the width of a golf ball perched at the end of a football field.

Regularity 5: Conditional Convergence Is Measurement Sensitive

Production and Consumption Measures

While there is ample room for alternative explanations, there can be no debate over the existence of conditional convergence across countries for income or consumption. The regularity of conditional convergence is so strong that it holds whether or not one adjusts income for imperfections in exchange rates or other estimation methods. Table 2.2 illustrates this by showing the correlations of various measures of income and consumption per capita, taken in absolute values or in logarithms. Whether adjusted for purchasing power parities or not, the correlations across measures are extremely high, exceeding .95 irrespective of the comparison — each variable reliably measures the other.[9] Although much discussion centers on estimation errors across countries (having some impact on aggregate measures and rankings), these differences are swamped by the long-run dynamics associated with conditional convergence.

In real terms, the most telling correlation is between income and private consumption (exceeding .95 in table

Table 2.2
Correlations across income measures

Absolute measure	(1)	(2)	(3)	(4)	(5)
(1) GDP per capita, PPP (current international $)	1.000				
(2) GNP per capita (constant 1995 US$)	0.944	1.000			
(3) GNP per capita, Atlas method (current US$)	0.951	0.999	1.000		
(4) GNP per capita, PPP (current international $)	0.998	0.952	0.957	1.000	
(5) Private consumption per capita (constant 1995 US$)	0.953	0.991	0.992	0.958	1.000
Log (absolute measure)	(1')	(2')	(3')	(4')	(5')
(1') Log GDP per capita, PPP (current international $)	1.000				
(2') Log GNP per capita (constant 1995 US$)	0.982	1.000			
(3') Log GNP per capita, Atlas method (current US$)	0.984	0.999	1.000		
(4') Log GNP per capita, PPP (current international $)	0.997	0.984	0.985	1.000	
(5') Log private consump. per capita (constant 1995 US$)	0.977	0.996	0.995	0.979	1.000

Source: Data for 1996, as reported in World Development Indicators, The World Bank, 1999; similar correlations exist for 1997 but substantially less countries are reported.

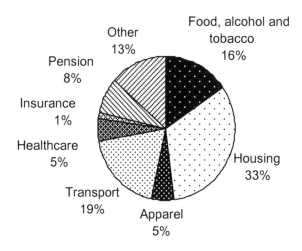

Figure 2.4
Consumption expenditures across items, United States, 1995

2.2). Conditional convergence in consumption makes this topic of practical importance. It is not that countries have different outputs per capita, they also consume vastly different amounts of food, housing, energy, transportation, entertainment, and other items. Without explanation, the differences appear staggering. Figure 2.4 breaks down consumption for the United States, as an example of a high-income country. Over 50 percent of income is dedicated to food, shelter, and clothing. While one might wish to believe that consumption in developed countries is largely associated with leisure and entertainment, a large part of work income is used to enhance fulfillment of basic needs or comfort. Furthermore, some percent of the remaining categories (e.g., transportation, health care) are dedicated to acquiring income to purchase these items or are part of basic need fulfillment.

Seen in this light, conditional convergence implies that steady-state levels of consumption for many broad categories are different from one country to another. Food consumption will be lower in the steady state in some countries than in others. Similarly for housing, clothing, and energy. By representing a large percent of consumption within all countries, the magnitude differences in these are as important to variances in total income across countries (i.e., high-income countries consume orders of magnitude more basic need items compared to low-income countries).

In this regard, one can explain conditional convergence by studying steady-state dynamics in production functions or the supply-side (assuming utility functions are homogeneous everywhere), or by studying steady-state dynamics in consumption (e.g., income generation may be endogenous to steady-state levels of consumption based on heterogeneous utility functions). Although both probably yield useful insights, the literature has almost exclusively relied on the former approach — irrespective of whether one refers to what Fogel calls the "old" or "new" schools of growth economics.

Convergence Fallacies

Measures of income and consumption are not studied for their own sake. Most texts in macroeconomics preface that these measures are highly associated with other more basic measures of well-being or utility fulfillment. Table 2.3 shows that this notion is largely born out by income's contemporaneous correlation with various consumption items and alternative measures of well-being: infant mortality, life expectancies, and literacy (access to written knowledge). Though the correlations vary in magnitude and significance, the association is manifest for both consumption and alternative measures of development.

Two fallacies arise, especially in popular circles, when considering such associations with conditional convergence. The first can be called a "correlation fallacy." Popularly, there is a false belief that if a development indicator is contemporaneously correlated to income, that the convergence dynamics of income implies the same dynamics for the other development measure. Though intuitive, there is no mathematical reason for this to be true. In fact, some development measures exhibit virtually the same convergence dynamics as income, while many others do not. This is true even though all of these measures show reasonably high contemporaneous correlations and are seen as being measures of similar things—economic development.

Table 2.3
Consumption correlations to income per capita

Consumption item	Correlation
Private consumption per capita (constant 1987 US$)	0.95
Telephone mainlines (per 1,000 people)	0.91
Vehicles (per 1,000 people)	0.88
Television sets (per 1,000 people)	0.79
Electric power consumption (kwh per capita)	0.79
Mobile phones (per 1,000 people)	0.75
Cable television subscribers (per 1,000 people)	0.70
Life expectancy at birth, total (years)	0.69
Radios (per 1,000 people)	0.44
Literacy rate, adult total (% of people 15+)	0.50
Mortality rate, infant (per 1,000 live births)	-0.64

Source and notes: Data are reported in World Development Indicators, 1999, the World Bank. All figures are for 1996, the latest year with most countries represented; income is measured as GDP per capita, PPP, 1996 US$. All correlations are statistically significant ($p\text{-}value<.01$).

Figures 2.5 and 2.6 illustrate the long-run convergence dynamics of infant mortality for time series collected across a reasonable number of countries, covering all latitudes, since the mid-1800s. Similar dynamics can be observed for life expectancy, literacy, and other related development measures (as discussed in chapter 8). Infant mortality and life expectancy are rather central economic variables given that one is fundamentally interested in utility maximization over consumers' time horizons, or life spans. The time horizon overwhelms most other considerations as premature death, especially in infancy, implies an enormous loss of welfare. Quality of life issues become academic when considering one person who lives two years and another who lives seventy-five years.

The data indicate β convergence for these alternative development indicators, despite these having a high contemporaneous correlation with income that exhibits conditional convergence (absolute divergence). For these, β convergence implies that σ approaches a steady state of zero. In other words, by focusing on divergences in income, one is focusing largely on that aspect of development mostly linked to the consumption of food, housing, clothing, transportation, entertainment, insurance, and health care (shown in figure 2.4), and not these other aspects of development. A complete model of growth would need to foresee the dynamics of both types of indicators.

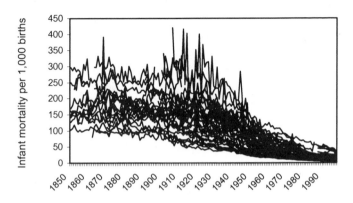

Figure 2.5
Infant mortality (deaths per 1,000 children to age one) across countries:
1850–1997

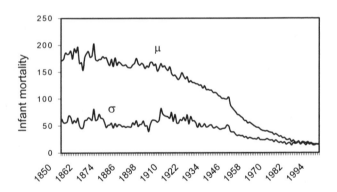

Figure 2.6
Infant mortality mean and standard deviation: 1850–1997 (adapted from
Mitchell 1998)

The second fallacy can be labeled the "basket fallacy of growth." By assuming that utility curves are everywhere invariant, as incomes rise all items in the basket should increase in a similar way across countries with similar levels of income (assuming similar supply efficiencies and international prices). In essence, when Singapore's income reaches the same level to that of Finland, the two should be consuming roughly the same types of products and services and in roughly the same quantities. It will be shown later that this will not be the case. Within convergence clubs that span latitudes, the paradox will reappear in the form of consumption heterogeneity. Physiological considerations would indicate divergence in consumption for items in the basket even if baskets have similar aggregate values across countries, provided these are located across latitudes. The basket fallacy lies in a popular belief that the world is becoming a global village with converging tastes and preferences, fostered by technology, ubiquitous media, information, or the internet. Integrating physical laws and physiology into macroeconomic consumption functions will largely dispel this ill-defined notion and provide predictions on the forms of variation likely to be seen in countries with similar incomes, yet receiving different levels of heat transfer, among other physical factors.

Regularity 6: Economic Growth Is Spatially Correlated, with Asymmetry

This regularity can be restated to say that conditional convergence is sensitive to the geographic boundaries limiting the sample of observations. Studies demonstrate that the closer the units of observation are to each other in geographic space, the less likely one is to observe conditional convergence. Sometimes called a "neighborhood effect," this regularity is revealed by looking at the income growth dynamics within countries or across countries in relatively small regions. In these cases, the data can indicate β convergence (or nearly so) with σ approaching a steady state value of close to zero from above. This contrasts sharply to a lack of β convergence and a large value of σ being approached from below in a broader sample of countries; see figures 2.2 and 2.3.

In Finland, for example, Kangasharju (1998) finds convergence in economic performance across the eighty-eight Finnish subregions from 1934 to 1993. Similar findings are reported in Barro and Sala-i-Martin (1995) for the U.S.A.; see also Persson (1995) for Sweden, Mas et al. (1995) for Spain, Barro and Sala-i-Martin (1995) for Japan, and Armstong (1995) for certain European regions. Neighborhood effects are rather commonplace in economic statistics. Moreno and Trehan (1997), for example, use a number of distance metrics to demonstrate a strong correlation in growth among neighboring countries. In their paper on the role of equipment investment on growth,

De Long and Summers (1991, p. 487) further note that "it is difficult to believe that Belgian and Dutch economic growth would ever significantly diverge, or that substantial productivity gaps would appear in Scandinavia." Explanations for this neighborhood effect include shared histories, overlapping cultures, knowledge spillovers, distribution interdependencies, or the instability of one's neighbors (e.g., Ades and Chua 1997).

As geographic boundaries are expanded, however, one begins to observe absolute divergence and the conditional convergence result. Figure 2.7 plots the growth dynamics of GNP per capita (in 1960 US$) for the period 1830 to 1970 across a sample of seventeen, mostly OECD and European countries, reported by Bairoch (1981); Maddison's sample provides identical results.[10] Because the sample contains sufficient representation from both northern and southern Europe (or distant neighbors), figure 2.8 shows a lack of β convergence, yet strongly indicates σ convergence approaching a steady state from a low initial starting condition. The countries on the top are the United States and Canada, whereas the country on the bottom is Portugal. Had the data been limited to only the Scandinavian regions, or to only the Mediterranean regions, however, the result is reversed and one observes absolute convergence, or neighborhood effects within these subregions.

Not unrelated to the equatorial paradox, it will now be shown how economic growth exhibits an asymmetric form

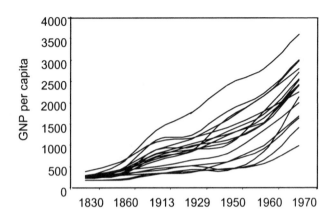

Figure 2.7
GNP per capita for seventeen countries (1960 USD): 1830−1970
(source: Bairoch 1981)

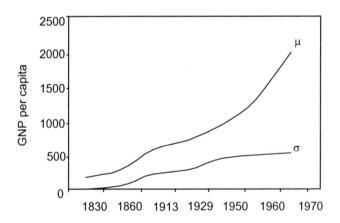

Figure 2.8
Mean GNP per capita and standard deviation for seventeen countries:
1830−1970 (source: Bairoch 1981)

of spatial correlation that will later be seen as germane to economic policy (chapter 7).

Detection

Broadly, there are two forms of spatial autocorrelation: positive and negative, as shown in figure 2.9. Negative spatial autocorrelation exists where two neighboring observations are dissimilar (a checkerboard). Positive spatial autocorrelation arises when two observations are neighbors in space and have similar development patterns. Similar in nature to the Durbin-Watson statistic in time series analysis, two statistics are commonly used to detect spatial autocorrelation: Moran's I and Geary's c. Moran's I, for example, varies in value from –1 to +1 and is calculated as a weighted product-moment correlation coefficient across n countries or "sampling stations."

Geary's c is similar but ranges generally from 0 to 2 with an expected value of 1 if spatial autocorrelation is absent, less than one if positive spatial correlation is present. Both measures rely on weights that capture proximity of the units considered (see Anselin 1986 for an exhaustive review).

While relatively common in studies of regional economics, these diagnostic statistics are rarely reported in models of cross-country economic growth that simply assume all countries are independent observations. The reason that spatial econometrics has yet to surface is due possibly to an

Negative spatial autocorrelation

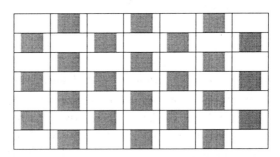

Positive spatial autocorrelation

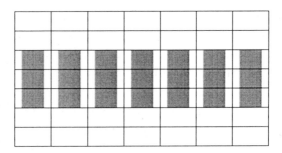

Figure 2.9
Spatial autocorrelation in cross-country studies

emphasis on within-country variations over time but also to a lack of widely available software programs able to handle the econometrics involved (e.g., SAS, SPSS, or TSP lack spatial econometric procedures).

Asymmetry

Two issues are involved in handling spatially correlated observations. The first is to realize what form it takes. The second is how to model it. In the first case, the problem is straight forward, but does include an element of art. In time series analysis, observations are separated typically by equal increments of time. In spatial econometrics one does not have this luxury. One is left to determine the $(n \times n)$ matrix of weights that are assigned by proximity. This can be distance in kilometers, say, or a distance class.

The Moran's I for international income statistics (across a variety of measures) varies in significance and sign depending on the distance metric used and the sample considered. It is highly significant and reveals positive spatial correlation if distances are limited to ranges generally below 1,500 kilometers and the data are limited to a given longitude (or range of longitudes, say, encompassing Europe and Africa).[11] If a country has a given level of income, it is more likely to have a neighbor of similar income than one that is randomly different. Moran's I also reveals negative spatial correlation if the distance is extreme and one aggregates income to the cluster of countries in wide zones. For example, northern

Europe has a dissimilar income to equatorial Africa, but a similar income to southern Africa.

Since the globe is spherical, one can replicate this finding for all longitudes. The implication is that spatial correlations are asymmetric: neighboring countries are similar, but more so by latitude than by longitude.

This asymmetry can be used to explain, for example, why De Long and Summers (1991) did not find spatial autocorrelations in the residuals of their growth model using absolute distances across countries. It is not the distances across each county that matters, but a country's distance from the equator. In spherical space, Australia is distant from the United States, yet in thermal space, it is a neighbor (hence the negative spatial correlation if one chooses a band which is 30 degrees latitude north and south of the equator). If latitude contributes to spatial correlation, one needs to focus on its direct effects.

Regularity 7: The Solar Climate

Despite the apparent absurdity in stating that the world's climates are empirical regularities, it is important to highlight a few subtle points if one is to consider the physiology of heat transfer. Climate, as opposed to weather, is viewed as average meteorological conditions that persist for a period of thirty years or more for a given geographic location. The degree to which one fine-tunes the definition of climate depends on the discipline. In climatology, a given climate can be decomposed by the causal mechanisms resulting in its variations across the earth's surface. From there, varieties can be defined, localized, mapped, and predicted. Since the purpose here is not to enter the debates that come with such classifications, one can simply note where there is general agreement (i.e., definitions).

Climates vary from one region to the next based on certain exogenous factors. The most exogenous of these is the solar climate, which is defined as the degree of latitude from the equator, or some nonlinear transformation of latitude. This factor captures two effects: the thermal radiation arriving on the earth's surface and the intensity of light. Figure 2.10 shows the effects of solar radiation for different times of the year at different latitudes (measured in calories received). If the earth had a uniform surface, one would find an almost symmetric climate above and below the equator, at equal absolute latitude. Topology and ocean currents (interacting with lunar and other cycles) interact to "perturb" the solar climate. For this reason, places around the globe can have similar latitudes but rather different climatic conditions. For instance, residents of Dallas, Texas, at 33°N latitude are used to receiving snow every year, with severe storms dropping up to 33cm in a period of 24 hours; average temperatures generally fall below 0°C every year, and many winters have temperatures falling to less than –15°C. In other parts of the world with similar or higher absolute latitudes, such extremes haven't been seen in the last 10,000 years (e.g., Bermuda, Sydney, Auckland, and Cairo).

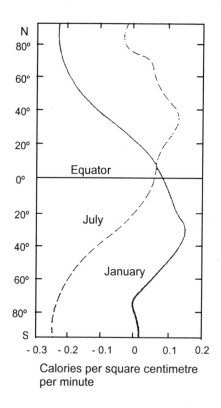

Figure 2.10
Natural caloric endowments (solar radiation)

Notes: Seasonal variation of heating of the atmosphere with latitude; intensity of net radiation received (adapted from Lamb 1977).

Similarly, the higher one's altitude, the more polar-like the climate, irrespective of the latitude (though these conditions are generally reached sooner the higher the absolute latitude). This effect generates for many countries or even the smallest islands, climatic potpourri. Crete, for example, has a Mediterranean climate in the coastal regions and an austere temperate climate in the mountain regions where annual snowfall is so high that residents are literally isolated from the rest of the island during the winter seasons; similar climatic variations are observed in Hawaii on the biggest island, and in Ecuador.

There is an asymmetry in the degree to which latitudes affect climate. Lower latitudes can experience temperate-like conditions (based on altitude), but higher latitudes rarely have tropical conditions, expect on exceptional days (record highs). Furthermore, lower latitudes, irrespective of altitude, will never experience wide seasonalities in temperature (though they often have rainy seasons), whereas temperate climates will never experience constant weather patterns. Likewise, the low angle of the sun in higher latitudes will never allow them to obtain the same average intensity of natural sunlight (concentration of photons) compared to the equatorial regions even though the former have very long summer days.

The word *climate* derives from the ancient Greek *klima*, or angle to the sun. Despite the numerous factors that determine a specific locality's climate, it turns out that a country's prevailing temperature is for the most part driven by latitude. Table 2.4 shows the correlation between latitude, a nonlinear transformation of latitude (its square), and a variety of temperature measures across 234 countries; the figures were weighted by the locational distribution of the population within each country — a factor important for the countries with large land areas or those spanning multiple latitudes (e.g., Russia, Brazil, the United States, Canada, India, Australia, and China). As shown, the table indicates that latitude is strongly correlated with average temperature, but also lower temperatures whether measured across the ranges of the monthly lows, or the lower ranges of the monthly highs. Latitude is not strongly correlated with the maximum levels of monthly highs throughout the year (i.e., the record highest temperature in each country).

In other words, all countries experience record highs that do not correspond to latitudes. Though typically for brief periods, one can observe over a thirty-year period an equatorially hot month, say, in European countries above 45°N latitude where monthly maximums over the last thirty years have surpassed 35°C. The reverse is not true, however. Over the last 5,000 years (or more) equatorial countries have not seen cold temperatures as found in Denmark (again, high altitude localities being the exception).

Table 2.4
Absolute latitude and temperature across 234 countries (Pearson correlations)

	Latitude	Latitude squared	Temperature °C	Temperature monthly high (min °C)	Temperature monthly high (max °C)	Temperature monthly low (min °C)	Temperature monthly low (max °C)
Latitude	1.00						
Latitude squared	0.97	1.00					
Temp: °C	-0.86	-0.88	1.00				
: monthly high (min °C)	0.85	-0.87	-0.94	1.00			
: monthly high (max °C)	0.01	-0.13	0.23	0.23	1.00		
: monthly low (min °C)	-0.88	-0.86	0.94	0.89	-0.07	1.00	
: monthly low (max °C)	-0.76	-0.79	0.88	0.78	0.21	0.82	1.00

Notes: Data provided in Parker (1997d).

In essence, using latitude as a explanatory variable one largely captures (1) the solar climate or the amount of solar energy received by the upper atmosphere, (2) the average temperature, (3) the number of photons reaching the earth's surface (luminosity), and (4) the degree to which thermal seasonality exists in a region (high, but not the highest latitudes have higher variances). In the grand scheme of things, latitude basically dominates all other climatic factors when considering all of the world's countries.[11]

Summary

Understanding how latitude might be related to the other empirical regularities so far noted will be the by-product of incorporating notions of physics and physiology into economic thinking. Doing so requires that certain basic fundamentals from these fields, especially relating to heat transfer, be considered in some detail. A task to which the book now turns.

Notes

1.   Rothman (1995, p. 22).

2.   This view of the equatorial paradox, based on supply-side considerations, was also detailed by Karamarck (1976) in a report for the World Bank.

3. Others, related specifically to the United States, are reviewed in Jones (p. 12−16) and Barro and Sala-I-Martin (1995, p. 5−9), but are less relevant to this discussion. In the United States over the last century: (1) the real rate of return to capital shows no trend (upward or downward); (2) the shares of income devoted to capital and labor show no trend, and (3) the average growth rate of output per person has been positive and relatively constant over time (i.e., the United States exhibits steady, sustained per capita income growth).

4. See, for example, the exchange between Lee et al. 1998 and Islam 1998.

5. Far more detailed discussions can be found in Barro and Sala-i-Martin (1992), Caselli et al. (1996), Cohen (1996), Evans (1996), Islam (1995), Jones (1995, 1997), and Quah (1993a, 1993b, 1996, 1997).

6. Bairoch (1981, p.10), adapted from Landes (1998, p. 232); figures for Spain and Czechoslovakia were back extrapolated for 1830 and 1860, respectively, to create a static sample, based on growth rates reported in Maddison (1995, p. 19−23).

7. Maddison's sample, in this regard, can be seen as a representative sample of all countries.

8. This is done by adding back one to the data to prevent taking a logarithm of zero.

9. The Cronbach alpha exceeds .80.

10. Moran's I is positive and statistically significant. Batteries of tests were performed in support of this paragraph using the software package C2D. The full reporting of the results do not lend themselves to this section but are easily replicated.

11. Deviations from this baseline effect can be captured by looking at the averages and variances in other climatic drivers (altitude, humidity, barometric pressure, marine temperature, wind conditions, prevalence of snowfall or frost, etc.). Alternatively, one can follow climatic categorization schemes and implement dummy variables or percent of surface area covered by type. Classification schemes range from those of Koppen to much more sophisticated satellite-based systems, among others. Data on these additional dimensions for all countries are given in Parker (1997d).

3   Utility Physics

One cannot logically be a determinist in physics and chemistry and biology, and a mystic in psychology.

— Donald Hebb

Over time, psychologists have come to recognize the importance of basic physical principles in explaining human psychological behaviors. This chapter covers elements in physics required to integrate certain natural sciences into economics. This in turn provides insights into the equatorial paradox among other topics of political economy. Following basic definitions, the chapter reviews how the law of energy conservation (especially heat transfer) affects all life on earth. The resulting mathematical relationships are then described for humans. These lead to rather precise physiological and psychological mechanisms, described in chapter 4, which act in a predictably divergent manner across countries.

Those educated in physics and neurophysiology might find the encyclopedic nature of this and the next chapter a bore. Without such an exposition, however, arguments that physical laws are somehow related to economics would appear ad hoc.

The brief treatment given to each topic is a function here of space limitations and cannot therefore reflect the wealth of insight offered by each. Physical processes other than energy conservation are certainly at work (e.g., gravity, friction, etc.), but they are less likely to impact cross-country variances in growth.

The Laws

A link between physical laws and economics can be made based on the infallible axioms that have made physics the most general science. Never proven, these fundamental laws are postulated and repeatedly demonstrated via experiment. Among the most enduring are the laws of conservation. Newton gave us the laws on the conservation of momentum and angular momentum. From Lavoisier we received the law on the conservation of matter. An entire movement of scientific inquiry in the late eighteenth century and early nineteenth century collectively gave what many believe is the greatest of all physical principles: the law of conservation of energy (thermodynamics). Other laws govern electric charges (Watson and Franklin), mass-energy (Einstein) and, more recently, subatomic conservation (e.g., charge, number of nucleon, number of baryons, number of leptons).

These physical laws serve scientific thought in three important ways. First, the laws set limits to all possibilities in all disciplines. To explain any observed phenomenon, one can quickly rule out violations of the laws. Second, the laws have general economic appeal. "You can't get something for nothing," and its corollary from the second law of thermodynamics "and you can't break even either," limit the realm of possibilities—e.g., there will never be a perpetual motion machine! Third, the laws demonstrate that no empirical observation can exist in contradiction to the collective laws at any level of analysis, whether considering subatomic processes, the workings of the human body, the dynamics of the solar system, or the organization of the cosmos. The laws have thus found direct applications to many fields of academic endeavor: astronomy, agriculture, engineering, and medicine.

Economic principles do not necessarily reflect violations of the laws of physics. The application of economics to a particular subject, however, faces the limits imposed by such laws as absolute. If not, then one must come up with more general laws or explanations for the observed violations. Probabilities can, however, crop up. In thermodynamics, for example, there are simply too many molecules to keep track of, though these are assumed to work in a deterministic way via Newtonian mechanics.[1] One can admit the possibility of a motionless object at rest spontaneously leaping into the air defying gravity. This event, however, is far "less likely than the probability that a group of monkeys typing randomly would by chance produce the complete works of Shakespeare."[2]

System Definition

Choosing the right law to focus attention on largely depends on the system studied. One can therefore spend less attention on how the laws govern the behaviors of, say, sub-atomic particles or gases (e.g., Boyles Law) and more on solid biological (chemical) entities. If the system is defined to include only the planet earth and all things on it, the laws would predict an instantaneous extinction of all life forms. Incomes per capita would converge to zero in all countries. By expanding the definition to include the sun, moon, and the remainder of the cosmos, one comes close to the situation we are in now. The system of study here, therefore, includes both humans and their solar environment.

Energy Conservation: A Primer

The laws most directly applicable to the governance of humans are the laws of thermodynamics. Feynman et al. (1963, p. 44−1) writes "The determination of the relationships among the various properties of materials, without knowing their internal structure, is the subject of thermodynamics. Historically, thermodynamics was developed before an understanding of the internal structure of matter was achieved." In a similar vein, this book considers the human body as a system without worrying too much about the processes going on at the atomic level.

The law of conservation of energy, or the first law of thermodynamics, is mostly attributed to Lavoisier and Joule.[3] It states that the various forms of energy can be transformed from one into another, but can neither be created nor destroyed (for a closed system):

$$\Delta U = \Delta W + \Delta Q \tag{3.1}$$

where ΔU is the change in internal energy, ΔW is work done by the system and ΔQ is heat added to the system. The internal energy of the system (U) is the sum of all forms of energy possessed by the atoms and molecules of the system: chemical, mechanical, electrical, thermal, light, and nuclear.[4]

It was not until the nineteenth century experiments of Joule (which replicated earlier unpublished experiments of Sadi Carnot), among others, that heat was understood as a transfer of energy. Joule's famous paddle wheel experiment linked work-energy to heat.

Work (W) is defined as the application of a force (f) over a given distance(d):

$$W = fd \tag{3.2}$$

For example, if one lifts a one-liter bucket of water ten meters, one exerts a force ($f = mg$ = 1 kg X 9.8 m/sec^2) over a distance of ten meters (h = 10 m), and does a certain amount of work ($W = mgh$ = 98 joules). Thus the internal energy U of the system (consisting of the bucket and its surroundings) is increased (by 98 joules). This energy can be recovered by pouring the water over a paddle wheel. Stored energy is often called potential energy. The energy of a moving object is called kinetic energy.

As water flows over a wheel, its potential energy is transformed into kinetic energy, which works on the paddle wheel, which churns a bucket of water, and the water is heated (Q). Heat was shown not to be a fluid (the *caloric* as imagined by Lavoisier), but rather is the ultimate form of energy resulting from transformation. In the late 1700s, Count Rumford (Benjamin Thompson) discovered this in his cannon boring factory by noticing that heat can be almost infinitely produced by using a blunt drill as long as the drill keeps turning.[5] The cannon does not store heat (as a fluid); rather, the mechanical energy of drilling is being transformed into heat.

Entropy and the Second Law of Thermodynamics

The entropy of a physical system is proportional to the logarithm of the number of microscopic, or internal, states that correspond to the macroscopic state. Heat is a function of entropy (S) and absolute (Kelvin) temperature (T).

Historically, entropy is defined in terms of the heat entering a system at a fixed temperature:

$$\Delta S = \Delta Q / T \tag{3.3}$$

Related to the first, the second law of thermodynamics can be stated in a number of equivalent manners:

- Heat flows spontaneously from hotter objects to colder objects, and never the opposite; or
- No heat engine that cycles continuously can change all of its heat to useful work; or
- A system's entropy will increase, or, at best, remain constant; or
- In isolated irreversible processes, some heat is always given off as waste (entropy increases); or
- "In the long run we are all dead." Keynes (1923, p. 65)

To be complete, one should mention the zeroeth and third law of thermodynamics. The zeroeth law states that if two objects are in thermal equilibrium with a third body, then the two objects are in thermal equilibrium with each other. Thermal equilibrium exists when all variables that describe the system are the same throughout the system. This concept more precisely defines "temperature"; when two objects are in thermal equilibrium with each other, they have the same temperature. The third law states that absolute zero temperature is not achievable.[6] Collectively, the laws of thermodynamics apply to all things, living or dead. Now, the laws will be narrowed to the living.

Conservation for Living Organisms

Academic disciplines apply the laws of thermodynamics somewhat differently given the nature of the systems studied and the environments surrounding these systems (e.g., materials science, versus biology).

The application of thermodynamics to living organisms is rather complex given their elaborate chemical and molecular structures. Very concisely, the chemical bonding among atoms involves the common sharing of electrons to form *molecules*. The attraction between the positive and negative charges of atoms provides the "glue" that prevents the atoms and molecules within living organisms from coming apart. Chemical bonds then permit the joining of multiple molecules into *substance*. All biological entities are comprised of cells that consist of similar chemical structures, but with variations in proportions and arrangements of these same *chemicals*. *Cells* are aggregated to the level of an *organism*. For the organism to survive, carbohydrates (carbon—water molecules), fat and protein are the principle nutrients — *the inputs* required on a daily basis. They do so by providing energy (fuel) and substance to insure the organism's integrity. With the exception of water and minerals, virtually all other substances found in the human body are comprised of carbon-based molecules.

Given the above, the implications of energy conservation on the human organism requires that the relevant system definition include the sun (i.e., the human body itself is not the correct system definition). The sun has a temperature of several million degrees. A portion of its potential energy is stored in the nucleus of hydrogen atoms, which is released via nuclear fusion. The resulting gamma radiation arrives to earth as radiant energy having traveled through a vacuum. In green plants, the pigment chlorophyll absorbs this radiant energy and transforms it to chemical potential energy of carbohydrates via the endergonic (energy storing) reactions known as photosynthesis.

This process results in a positive free energy change:

Chlorophyll

$$6CO_2 + 6H_2O \longrightarrow 6O_2 + \text{carbohydrates} + \text{standard free energy (686 cal/mole)}$$

Light Energy

In essence, solar radiation and photosynthesis supply carbohydrates, oxygen (used by animals for energy metabolism), and free-standing energy that is consumed by animals who breath, and eat nutritious vegetation (or other animals who are lower on the food chain). Digested plants are, therefore, the first-order store of potential energy that can be converted to fats and proteins for current and future animal use. Transformation continues in animals that exploit this potential energy and produce waste heat in performing mechanical work (muscle contraction), chemical work (biosynthesis of cellular molecules), and transport work (concentrating chemicals in fluids). The chemical reaction involved in respiration (an exergonic process), for example, shows a negative standard free energy change:

$$C_6H_{12}O_6 + 6O_2 \longrightarrow 6CO_2 + 6H_2O \text{ – standard free}$$
$$\text{energy (686 kcal/mole)}$$

The laws of conservation, therefore, demonstrate that without the exogenous useable energy from the sun (food via photosynthesis and oxygen) there would be no animal life of earth. Having covered all living things, the chapter now narrows the discussion to humans.

Human Energy Conservation: Origins

The application of energy conservation laws to humans quickly followed the basic laws discovered by Lavoisier, Joule and Carnot, among others.[7] Humans are homeotherms and must maintain an internal core temperature within a relatively narrow range near 37°C. The extension of conservation laws to human behaviors is found in the literature on body temperature and thermoregulation.[8] The early pioneers who noted a relationship between temperature and physiology include Hippocrates (460 B.C.), Alexandrinus (100 B.C.), Galileo (1603), who invented the first "thermoscope," and Santorio

(1615), who invented the thermo-"meter." Progress came with the superior instruments of thermometry, the modern versions of which find their origins in the work of de Medici (1667), Fahrenheit (1724), and Kelvin (1848). In medicine, an important pause occurred after Boerhaave (1709) introduced the concept of heat measurement in diagnosing illness, as the next 150 years saw this concept languish. In chemistry, however, Lavoisier et al. (1782) made great advances. Despite the premature death via decapitation of Lavoisier, his thoughts and experiments gave us the concepts of metabolism, biological oxidation, and chemical energy or work—the modern sciences of chemistry and physiology.

The breakthrough notion of human thermoregulation, or a direct link between physics and human behavior, can be traced to a little known letter from Benjamin Franklin (1758) to a physician in South Carolina. In it, Franklin reports certain of his experiments showing that sweating is a manner by which the body eliminates excess heat. Combined with Lavoisier's discovery of chemical metabolism and the idea of a stable *milieu interieur* from Claude Bernard (1876) came the idea of homeostatic equilibrium. Before Bernard, temperature was an ill-understood parameter in medicine—a field that now uses it as a universal diagnostic tool. After Bernard, the world came to recognize the "energy conservation law" for humans as *thermal homeostasis* (Benzinger 1967).

A modern mathematical description of the physics regulating human energy conservation was given by Montheith (1973) at the University of Nothingham is his book *Principles of Environmental Physics*. From this work and a number of others since, a rather complete physical explanation of human energy conservation has now been developed (see Stanier et al. 1984). This proved to be no minor challenge for humans because our bodies are not a homogenous system, i.e., they are not comprised of a uniform substance or set of molecules. Furthermore, we are able to adjust to our environment using a complex combination of autonomic and behavioral responses. Some of these behavioral responses are "man-made" or economic in nature.

Human Energy Conservation: Specification

Like all irreversible processes, the human body gives off waste heat. Typical to homeothermic mammals, we have relatively minor changes in internal heat (ΔQ is nearly 0). Although limited variation can exist around this equilibrium for brief periods of time, the body is regulated to minimize this variation. If regulation breaks down or is insufficient, the organism suffers or can perish (e.g., from hypothermia or heat stroke); entropy then accelerates as indicated in equation 3.3 above. The law of energy conservation is typically translated into the following energy balance equation for humans:

Energy production = Work + (Heat Loss) + Storage   (3.4)

Physics demonstrates that heat can only be transferred by a combination of radiation, evaporation, convection, and conduction: $Q = f(R, E, Cv, Cd)$; equation 3.4 can be formally stated as (deltas have been dropped to conform with convention in physiology):

$$M = W + (R + E + Cv + Cd) + S \qquad (3.5)$$

where M is the metabolic rate (heat production), W is heat loss/gain via mechanical work (e.g. shivering), R is heat/gain loss due to radiation, E is evaporation rate, Cv is the loss/gain rate due to convection, and Cd is the loss/gain rate due to conduction. S is the rate of heat storage in tissues. The heat exchange equation 3.5 directly follows, therefore, from equation 3.1 which expresses the law of energy conservation. It recognizes that humans exchange energy with the environment. Coupled with the notion that we have genetically evolved to maintain a homeostatic core body temperature of 37°C, equation 3.5 is probably the single most important mathematical description of human existence in terms of causally describing our core consumption behaviors. To more precisely describe the implications of this equation, we now turn to each of its components. In what follows, I will summarize the physics of this process but delegate mathematical descriptions to the end notes.

Energy Production: Metabolism (M) and Work (W)

To maintain an internal temperature of 37°C, humans produce heat using metabolic processes. Our primary source of energy is the heat by-product generated from the catabolism of food. Cryptically, food is broken down in such a way that chemical energy contained in nutrients are stored in the mitochondria (sausage-like capsules which are most numerous in cells performing a high level of metabolic activity). Within the mitochondria, energy is stored in ATP molecules (adenosine triphosphate) that can be thought of as the body's "currency" spent to buy work at the cellular level (movement, secretion, and synthesis). A series of chemical reactions specify this process. In the first, the ATP molecule is split yielding ADP (adenosine diphosphate), phosphate and energy spent, for example, to contract a muscle. This is represented in equation 3.6 as:

$$ATP \longrightarrow ADP + P_i \qquad\qquad (3.6)$$

The ADP molecule is quickly restored to ATP (rephosphorylated) by a high-energy phosphate group from a creatine phosphate molecule. At the molecular level, this chemical reaction adheres to the law of conservation of matter and energy. All used energy stored in food is released by such oxidation-reduction reactions, its generic form being given in Houdas and Ring (1982, p. 12):

$$AH_2 \quad + \quad B \quad \longrightarrow \quad A \quad + \quad BH_2 \quad + \quad Energy$$

Substance to be Oxidized (potential energy)	Substance to be Reduced (generally CO_2)	Substance Oxidized (generally CO_2)	Substance Reduced	To be captured and or transformed

Using a calorimetric bomb, Houdas and Ring 1982, (p. 13 – 14) report the following mean values for energy released for a variety of foods (in kJ/100g):

Food	Type	Energy produced
Leafy vegetables	Vegetable	55
Tomatoes	Vegetable	110
Green and yellow	Vegetable	140
Citrus fruits	Vegetable	160
Other fresh fruits	Vegetable	200
Potatoes	Vegetable	305
Poultry, fish	Animal	555
Eggs	Animal	610
Meat	Animal	975
Bread	Vegetable	1150
Cheese	Animal	1255
Flour and cereal products	Vegetable	1530
Dry beans and peas	Vegetable	1785
Butter	Animal	3030

In the human body, energy production parallels that of caloric bombs, though the energy cannot be totally used since intestinal absorption does not affect all substance molecules equally. Below are Houdas and Ring's (p. 13) estimates of energy production across three broad classes of substances (in kj/gr of substance):

Substance	Total	Energy from metabolism	Effective absorption
Glucose	17.55	17.55	17.15
Protein	23.40	19.85	17.15
Lipid (fats/oils)	39.30	39.30	37.60

From these food groups, catabolic processes liberate three forms of energy: chemical storage, work, and metabolic heat. A person's metabolic rate is the quantity of food energy effectively converted in a given unit of time. The human body is approximately 20 percent efficient. At maximum efficiency, some 20 percent of human ingested food energy is available for work, while the remaining 80 percent is heat energy. If a human is at full rest, then 100 percent of food energy eventually appears as heat (food energy = heat).

Where the heat is anatomically produced varies depending on physical activity, Wenger and Hardy (1990, p. 150 – 178) report the following for human heat production when exercising and when at rest:

Body area	Body mass %	Heat production (%) Rest	Exercise
Brain	2	16	1
Trunk viscera	34	56	8
Muscle and skin	56	18	90
Other	8	1	1
Total	100	100	100

A number of factors affect the release of energy from food across individuals including demographics (age, gender), physical appearance (body size), level of activity (exercise, shivering), the environment (temperature, climate), and stress (disease, fever, emotional state). Labor produces various amounts of energy depending on the activity. All other factors held constant, professional activities (e.g., writing) increase metabolic rates by some 500 Calories per day, moderate work (e.g., strolling) by 1000 Calories per day, hard labor (e.g., ditch digging) by 4,800 per day (Rhoades and Pflanzer 1996, p. 807)[9]:

Activity	Energy (calories/hour)
Sitting	100
Walking slowly	200
Intercourse	280
Swimming	500
Jogging	325
Rowing	825

Comparing raw metabolic rates across individuals proves problematic due to the fact that body weight and muscle mass (which often varies by gender) is not constant. If measured on a per gram or surface area basis, however, metabolic rates become acceptably comparable. The notion of a basal metabolic rate (BMR) has evolved over time and, from a law of conservation point of view, is the closest thing to an "absolute cost of living" index.

The BMR is typically measured in the morning (metabolic rates are greatest in the late afternoon; Mackowiak et al. 1992) on a subject who has fasted for 12 hours and has remained at rest for at least 30 minutes in a comfortable room heated to 25°C. In these conditions, persons with very different body masses, or genders, may have different metabolic rates, but can be compared on the same "cost of living index." It is common to measure metabolism using a respirometer that measures net oxygen consumption. When one liter of oxygen oxidizes carbohydrates, 5 Calories of energy are released; 4.7 Calories for fat and 4.6 Calories for protein (Rhoades and Pflanzer 1996, p. 810).[10]

While heavier humans will generally exhibit higher metabolic rates, the rate is not directly related to mass but rather is roughly proportional to surface area.

All things remaining equal, equation 3.5 implies that if external temperatures vary, one might expect differences in food consumption patterns by temperature range. This is not obvious, however, as one can compensate for external temperature using various components from the right-hand side of the equation, now discussed.

Heat Dissipation

Physical and chemical mechanisms by which heat is generated and dissipated are fairly well understood. Following ingestion, the *specific dynamic action* of foods increases heat production: an average meal containing a higher percentage of carbohydrates and fats increases metabolism by 4 percent while the same meal containing large quantities of protein increase metabolism by up to 30 percent. Most of the heat appears to originate in the chemical reactions of the liver. Heat is then transported via the circulatory system to the body's outer shell or skin tissues where it cools.

Under hard labor conditions, if the body were unable to release the heat generated, the body's core temperature increases by some 4°C per hour; brain lesions and heat stroke then precede death. Unlike fish and reptiles (poikilotherms), humans cannot survive wide variations in core body temperature and must somehow regulate temperature via physiological and behavioral responses. The laws of physics dictates that M be offset, as specified in equation 3.5. The remaining components of the human heat exchange equation mostly relate to the interface between the skin, where blood circulates, and the environment. Here, each component is summarized by its general order of importance, in descending order.

Energy Loss: Radiation *(R)*

From the second law of thermodynamics given in equation 3.3, one knows that the heat always transfers from a warm body to a cooler body. Ultimate entropy in humans is death. A nude human sitting calmly in a room heated to 21°C losses some 60 percent of her heat via radiation (Rhoades and Pflanzer 1996). Broadly defined, radiation can come from any surface (e.g., a fire's flame is a surface) and can travel through a vacuum (e.g., solar radiation to the earth). One can think of radiation as two distinct kinds:

short-wave and long-wave. Short-wave radiation comes in wavelengths measuring from $0.3\mu m$ to $3\mu m$. Hot fires and the sun emit short-wave radiation. Long-wave radiation (approximately $5\mu m$ to $100\mu m$) is emitted by all living beings who are also on the receiving end of short-wave radiation. Bodies emitting short-wave radiation can either gain or lose heat depending on the emitting properties of the surrounding surfaces.

With the heat-exchange equation 3.5, one is interested in the net transfer from and to line-of-sight surroundings. A number of factors affect this exchange, including orientation. For example, a person standing in front of a chimney fire is mostly exposed to the heat of radiation, while the warmer air that might affect convection rises up the flu. The person will absorb radiant heat on the side exposed to the fire (e.g., the front), while the person's back will be losing radiating heat to the environment (and hence feel cooler).

The variations of skin colors for humans and other mammals have proven paradoxical. Why is it that polar bears have white coats when the above would suggest that they should be black? Mitchell (1974) gives part of the explanation, at least for polar bears:

> Just as black is a surprising color for desert animals, white would seem to be thermally unfavorable for polar animals. Their white coats are generally considered to have evolved not because they favor energy balance, but because they favor camouflage in the snow. However, what appears white to human eyes may well appear otherwise to the eyes of animals more sensitive to the ultraviolet, as Lavigne and Oritsland have shown by photographing polar bears in the ultraviolet region of the spectrum. Polar bears are apparently "black" to ultraviolet radiation, and absorption of the ultraviolet part of solar radiation may, therefore, contribute to their energy balance.

R captures heat transfer via electromagnetic radiation between objects that are not in physical contact. The color of a surface has no relevance to long-wave radiant heat exchange; here emissivity matters. Emissivity of a surface is equal to it absorbidity, or the fraction of incident radiant energy that the surface absorbs (ideal emitters are called black bodies).[11] Few surfaces reflect low-wave radiant heat; the exception being highly polished metals. The use of aluminum-foil blankets for neonates, survival kits, and astronauts thus increase the retention of the body's radiant energy. At approximately 35°C, there may be net heat gain via radiation. This is a rare occurrence for the average human since few places are inhabited with such high average temperatures (Djibouti has one of the highest average prevailing temperatures at 30°C).[12]

All factors held constant, the equation specifying radiation exchange demonstrates that as environmental radiant temperatures increase to high levels, humans will have to engage in a strategy to avoid or block this radiation (e.g., seek "shade"). Where temperatures fall below a certain threshold, however, one seeks to minimize loss or increase our absorption of natural or artificial radiation (where heat dissipation is great and food metabolism alone can not maintain core temperature). Findings from various studies (military and others) estimating the impact of this physical process on the utility of certain forms of clothing and housing are considered in chapter 6.

Energy Loss: Evaporation *(E)*

For people resting in comfort, the amount of water evaporation is some 600 ml per day and represents about 20 percent of the total heat transfer process (Rhoades and Pflanzer, 1996, p. 812). Physiologists refer to this as *insensible perspiration* as it generally occurs with the person being unaware of the process. Sweating is the active physiological process of water secretion by sweat glands in the skin. Sweating is a physiological reaction to overheating. Secretion increases linearly with body temperature. When exposed to very hot environments, the only option for the body is to evaporate sweat (conduction and radiation at high temperatures increase body temperature). Under extreme conditions, the body can sweat 1.5 liters of water per hour and can evaporate in optimal conditions 800 Calories of body heat per hour (or twelve times basal metabolic heat production). In hot environments, the body's ability to evaporate decreases with humidity. Evaporation heat loss, E, is almost always positive.[13] The often-noted exception is in a steam room (or Swedish sauna) where heat is transferred to the body by condensing water vapor on the skin. Fundamentally, evaporation is the process of converting a liquid to a gas. Thermal energy is required for such a transformation. In the case of humans, when 1 gram of water evaporates from the body, approximately .58 Calories of heat are transferred from the skin. For humans, this process is continual as small quantities of water evaporate from the skin, respiratory tracts and mucous membranes of the mouth.

Similarly to radiation, the implication of equation 3.5 is that as ambient temperatures-humidity rise, one compensates by encouraging perspiration (e.g., wearing less or no clothing, using architecture that encourages flowing air currents, etc.). All other factors held constant, opposite strategies are required for cold ambient temperatures, where heat dissipation from evaporation will be discouraged (e.g., from layered clothing and appropriate architecture).

Energy Loss: Convection (*Cv*)

Convection is the loss of heat energy from a warmer to a cooler region via the movement of a fluid (water or air). Convection can result from the free flowing of air (e.g., the wind) or be man-made (via central heating, air-conditioning, etc.). For a given individual, when the ambient temperature drops, the greater the heat loss, all other factors being held constant.[14] Clothing can effectively reduce convection on nonnaked surfaces by trapping a layer of air between the skin and the garment that creates an artificial pocket of ambient temperature.[15]

One would also expect in areas with sufficiently high ambient temperature, the use of lighter clothing, perhaps simultaneously encouraging evaporation that might be used to encourage convective heat loss. In regions where temperatures drop low enough, layered clothing is likely. Similarly for architecture, forced air heating, and cooling.

Energy Loss: Conduction (*Cd*)

Heat exchange via conduction results from kinetic energy among molecules of objects that are in direct physical contact with the skin. The term *Cd* is therefore restricted to the flow of heat between the physical body and other immediately adjacent objects. On balance, conduction generally proves to represent a minor percent of heat dissipation (or gain). When a person is standing, the principle place where conduction takes place is through the soles of the feet. When in bed, heat loss is generally low given the types of materials that make up bed surfaces. When on the ground, heat loss can be high. The principles of conduction are most frequently noticed in extreme physical conditions. When the body is laid in a cold lake, for example, heat loss is rapid as water conducts heat twenty times more effectively than air. The literature on hypothermia, environmental physiology, and sports medicine focuses on these extreme cases.

Mathematically, conduction, Cd, follows the general relationship proposed by Fourier in 1822.[16] Intuitively, conduction depends on the object and the skin that contacts the object. The amount to which heat is transferred is a function of the product of the object's conductivity, density, and specific heat (a constant). Because the product of three factors comes into play in defining the conductive heat-transfer coefficient, one often finds that the temperature of an object does not necessarily relate to the sensation of it being "cold" or "hot." For example, a piece of metal cooled to $0°C$ will seem much cooler to the touch than a piece of wood. In fact, the two objects have the same temperature; we simply are losing heat more rapidly to the metal thus making our fingers cool more rapidly.

All other factors held constant, one would expect to see in places of sufficiently high temperatures, steady-state consumption of items encouraging conductive heat loss (e.g., tile, or earth-based flooring in warmer regions). In regions with sufficiently low temperatures, one would expect steady-state consumption discouraging conductive heat loss (e.g., wooden flooring).

Energy Storage (S)

Heat storage is the energy balance residual: heat produced — gained less heat loss. Storage is assumed to be negligible for most studies of humans. Prolonged positive storage (obesity) is now recognized as a disease, genetic predisposition, or long-run cultural trait (World Health Organization 1998). The amount of heat stored depends on body mass, the body's mean specific heat, and the mean body temperature. The mean specific heat of the body depends on its composition, and in particular, the proportion of fat present. The mean body temperature depends on ambient temperature, the core body temperature, and the skin temperature. Stored energy in tissues changes their temperatures. Storage is typically called upon when the body is under stress; in most discussions of animal thermoregulation it is assumed to equal zero as it only is called upon during temporary intervals ($S \approx 0$).[17] Again, for homeotherms, one generally does not expect to see storage as a critical component to heat exchange.

Summary

The energy balance equation now fully specified, one sees how the laws of physics have been translated to animals and to humans in particular. Figure 3.1 summarizes the

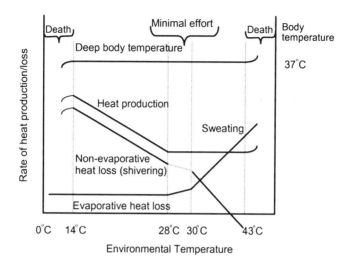

Figure 3.1
Environmental temperature and thermoregulatory effort

Note: Adapted from Stanier et al. 1984, p. 17, and Rhodes and Tanner 1995, p. 596. The temperatures in the figure above are for an unclothed adult male acclimatized to a temperate climate. Between 28°C and 30°C one obtains the thermoneutrality, or is the "zone of least thermoregulatory effort", whereby heat loss occurs via imperceptible evaporation, and not active sweating. Similar zones exist for infants, women, and residents of the tropics, but these exist at higher temperature levels.

behavioral aspects of human thermodynamics (Stanier et al. 1984). As shown, physiological effort is minimized in the ambient temperature range between 28°C and 30°C. As temperatures fall, heat production must increase. Above this range, sweating takes place. This range exists for humans at rest acclimated to the low-effort range. For social reasons, one generally tends to wear minimal clothing and be mobile. For these reasons, as elaborated in the next chapter, the temperature of minimal effort in practice begins at a lower temperature, approximately 25°C. This threshold varies according to one's acclimatization; an autonomic process subject to the temperature range that the body is normally exposed to on a daily basis. Therefore, visitors from temperature regions feel uncomfortable in the tropics, compared to residents, unless they have lived there long enough to acclimatize. If there for short periods, temperate residents can comfortably live in the tropics relying on artificial environments replicating a temperate climate (similarly for tropical residents relocating to colder regions, but in reverse). For residents in the few regions of the world where the body has difficulty acclimatizing in a permanent manner, due to extreme seasons (Siberian winters and tropical summers), the physiological demand for artificial compensation is highest. Research has revealed that as the temperature falls low enough, effort to achieve thermal balance (comfort) via autonomic and/or economic adaptation increases exponentially.

The next chapter describes the critical neurological mechanisms within the human body that make thermoregulation and utility maximization possible. It shows that the resulting physiology leads to chemical homeostasis, or homeostatic utility. From there, one can infer preference structures and predict steady-state consumption patterns for broad classes of goods and services which, when aggregated, lead to similar qualities of life (comfort) with predictably divergent standards of living.

Notes

1. Quantum mechanics and Heisenberg's uncertainty principle lead one to a chaotically deterministic view of the world, at least at the level of an electron. This uncertainty is compounded by statistical uncertainties.

2. Giancoli (1989, p. 497).

3. See Ericksen (1998) for an in-depth summary.

4. More precisely, energy (U) is defined as the ability to do work. Work (W) in turn is defined as the application of a force (f) over a given distance (d):

$$W = fd$$

From Newton one knows that force is mass (m) times acceleration (a); substituting into the equation above one finds that work is mad:

$$W = mad$$

One also knows that objects falling from height h being accelerated by gravity g to produce work:

$$W = mgh$$

An object has a potential energy, therefore, based on its position (height from the center of the earth). Once dropped it travels a distance (d) and reaches velocity (V) generating kinetic energy:

$$V^2/2 = ad$$

By substitution, one obtains the "work-energy" theorem:

$W = 1/2mV^2$

The total energy of an object is the sum of its potential and kinetic energies.

5. See Wilson (1960) for an interesting summary of his life and experiments.

6. The third law equivalently states that entropy of a pure crystalline substance can be taken to be zero at the absolute temperature of $0°$ Kelvin.

7. Whittow (1970), Satinoff (1980), and Johnston and Bennett (1996) provide broad coverage of other animal species (invertebrates, nonmammalian vertebrates, and nonhuman mammals).

8. A required reading for those interested in understanding the history of the application of laws of conservation to humans are the two volumes entitled *Temperature* edited by Benzinger (1977a, 1977b). These texts reproduce the original and translated texts of this field's greatest thinkers.

9. The convention of physiologists and nutritionists are followed here by using Calories (capital C, or kilocalorie), as opposed to calories (small c) as used in physics or chemistry; the difference being the heat required to increase 1 kg, versus 1 g, of pure water $1°C$.

10. Frequently the energy released from these foods are averaged to obtain the simple conversion:

$M = [O_2 \ (l/hr)(4.825 \ Calories/lO2)]/[surface \ area \ (m2)]$

11. Excluding behavioral adjustments, the extent to which the human skin emits radiation is proportional to the fourth power of skin temperature and follows Stefan-Boltzmann's law:

$R = \sigma \varepsilon_s T_{sk}{}^4$

where σ is the Stefan-Boltzmann constant (derived from Planck's law), T_{sk} is skin temperature, and ε_s is skin emissivity.

The emissivity of human skin depends on the wavelength considered. Thermal radiation is mostly in the infrared range for human tissues and ambient temperatures. In the infrared (near 9.5μm), human skin emissivity approaches 1 or that of a blackbody (irrespective of skin color). The behavioral version of this equation can be expressed as:

$R = h_r\, e_{sk}\, A_r\, (T_{sk} - T_r)$

where h_r is the radiant heat transfer coefficient, e_{sk} is the emissivity of skin (0< e_{sk} <1), A_r is the radiating skin surface, and T_r is absolute temperature of the radiant environment. A_r depends on the person's posture (a spread-eagle stance maximizes heat transfer while a crouch minimizes this transfer). The heat transfer coefficient, h_r, depends on the ambient temperature; at 28ºC, h^r =6.43W/(m^{2}ºC).

12. Parker (1995, p. 19).

13. Evaporative heat loss from the skin to the environment, E, can be characterized by the following:

$E = h_c A_w (P_{sk,sat} - P_a)$

where h_c is an evaporate heat loss constant, A is the surface area of the skin, w is the skin wettedness coefficient, and $(P_{sk,sat} - P_a)$ is the difference between the saturation water vapor pressure at skin temperature, and the ambient water vapor pressure.

14. The rate at which convection occurs can be expressed as follows:

$Cv = h_{cv}A(T_{sk} - T_a)$

where h_{cv} is a convection heat-transfer coefficient, A is the body surface area, and $(T_{sk} - T_a)$ is the difference between mean skin temperature (T_{sk}) and ambient temperature (T_a). The heat-transfer coefficient incorporates a number of factors. As the radius of skin curvature decreases, h_{cv} increases; this curvature explains why hands and feet are highly convective despite having relatively small skin areas. Convection resulting from air movement around the skin is the most important factor for humans affecting h_{cv} and has been found to vary approximately to the square root of wind speed.

15. See Barton and Edholm (1955).

16. Cd depends on skin temperature, T_s, the temperature of the object, T_{ob}, and the area of contact, A_k:

$Cd = h_k A_k (T_s-T_{ob})$

where h_k is the conductive heat-transfer coefficient which in turn is a function of the object's conductivity k, density ρ, and specific heat c.

17. Heat storage can be represented by:

$S = m q \Delta T_b / t$

where S is measured in Calories per hour, m is mass in kilograms, q is a specific heat coefficient (approximately 0.83 in humans), ΔT_b is the change in temperature, and t is time in hours.

4   Utility Physiology

Summertime, and the living is easy.

— From *Porgy and Bess* (Gershwin)

While physics alone can tell us all we need to know about human energy balance, it can be useful to understand the details of how the human organism fulfills energy conservation. How is it that our body motivates us to work to obtain various goods and services, especially those meeting basic needs (e.g., food, shelter, clothing)? The story must center on brain functions and a good starting point is the hypothalamus. If the hypothalamus did not exist, the laws of physics would require that something like it be invented. In essence, the physical laws of chapter 3 lead to complex interactions involving the hypothalamus which in turn affects chemical homeostasis in the body via hormones, neurotransmitters, and other chemical substances. From chemical homeostasis, one will later infer functional forms and variances in utility functions and consumption functions for a large enough number of goods and services to demonstrate that ignoring this biological reality becomes hazardous in cross-country economic studies.

History of the Human Thermostat

Even as recently as 120 years ago, the idea that thermoregulation depends on a neurological function was not known. Lavoisier with his student and experimental subject Armand Seguin (1785) espoused a rather intuitive idea based on respiration –- the lungs are the origin of heat regulation. As we breathe air, the lungs are the source of oxygen that enters all heat-generating oxidation processes. When we exhale, carbon is bonded to oxygen and then released to the atmosphere. The respiratory system therefore must be the source of energy regulation. Claude Bernard (1876) refuted this belief, finding instead that the source of heat regulation likely resided in neurological mechanisms.

While Bernard did not identify the exact location of these mechanisms (due to a lack of precise measurement instruments and methods), his research presented an important by-product: the idea that controlled experiments in medicine were possible. Up to the late nineteenth century, the world believed that humans were far too complex and sensitive to factors such as culture, ethnicity, and socioeconomics to achieve a universal medicine; e.g., experiments performed on or knowledge gained from poor persons residing in one part of a city (or place of the world) might not be applicable to the rich. Bernard rejected this and lectured that human physiology behaves in a universally and experimentally predictable fashion, provided that proper controls for exogenous factors are accounted for and measured with precision.

On the shoulders of Bernard, two medical students in Berlin in 1885 discovered the approximate location of the "human thermostat." Eduard Aronsohn and Julius Sachs (1885) were not the first to think that the more primitive portions of the brain might be the origin of temperature regulation. They achieved notoriety, however, by their precision using a "piqûre" method applied to the brains of rabbits. Beyond any doubt, they discovered a critical yet tiny sensory organ, a literal "needle in the haystack" near the end of the brain stem, what is now known as the preoptic-supraoptic area in the hypothalamus. The experiments were performed under what today would appear to be rather crude conditions: no anesthesia, no thermally isolated rooms, and no cotton packing of the subjects. A needle of 3 mm was thrust into the brain and immediately removed after the cranial cavity was exposed from a split in the dura mater. A small piece of cotton soaked in carbolic acid was then placed on the wound before being closed with a suture. Body temperature was measured in the rectum at a depth of 7mm. The animals remained alive for three to four days after which their brains were studied to locate the precise locations of the piqûre which were matched to measured temperature variations.

Some twenty-seven years later, Isenshmid and Krehl (1912), using transections of the brain stems of rabbits, dogs, and guinea pigs, found a second hypothalmic heat center. The second is associated with total thermoregulatory failure when transection takes place in that hypothalmic region of the brain stem. Earlier results were disputed as the unsanitized instruments involved may have themselves resulted in the heat changes (e.g., fevers) observed. Modern regulatory physiology and an understanding of autonomic functions nevertheless were born from these experiments that stood up to modern research methods.[1]

Recent Findings

The hypothalamus is located near the base of the brain. This region is considered a primitive area of the brain and can be found in many lower form mammals. Evolution in human ancestors gave us this high-precision servomechanism sensitive to rather minute changes in stimuli. Containing a number of distinct nuclei, it has widespread connections with the forebrain and the midbrain. Interconnected to the loosely defined limbic system via these nuclei and fiber tracts, hypothalmic connections reach areas of the brain directly associated with emotions, motivation, and various kinds of memory.

Rhodes and Tanner (1995, p. 129) provide the following medical description:

> The hypothalamus coordinates autonomic reflexes of the brainstem and spinal cord. It also activates the endocrine and somatic motor systems when responding to signals generated either within the hypothalamus or brainstem or in higher centers, such as the limbic system, where emotions and motivations are generated. The hypothalamus can accomplish this by virtue of its unique location at the interface of the limbic system with the endocrine and autonomic nervous systems.

Rhodes and Tanner (1995, p. 129) also provide a summary of its role in thermoregulation and homeostasis in general:

> The hypothalamus is a major regulator of homeostasis. Capillaries in the hypothalamus, unlike other brain blood vessels, possess a "leaky" blood-brain barrier, which allows the cells of hypothalmic nuclei to sample freely, from moment to moment, the composition of extracellular fluid. It then initiates the mechanisms necessary to maintain levels of regulated constituents at a given set point, which is itself fixed within more or less narrow limits by a specific nucleus of the hypothalamus. Homeostatic functions regulated by the hypothalamus include body temperature, water and electrolyte balance, and plasma glucose

level. The hypothalamus is the major regulator of
the endocrine system by virtue of its connections
with the pituitary gland, the master gland of the
endocrine system.

Because of its relationship to "spectacular effects, the rather
small hypothalamus attracts more than its share of
attention from biological psychologists" (Kalat, p. 87). An
early summary of the state of knowledge covering
hypothalmic functions is presented in three volumes edited
by Morgane and Panksepp (1980). Neurophysiologists and
biological psychologists have investigated the central role
of the hypothalamus by observing behaviors in
experimental subjects (mostly animals) and/or psychiatric
patients having damage to hypothalmic nuclei. Behaviors
include thirst, hunger, sexuality, sleep cycles, aggressivity,
and mood.

Hypothalmic Chemistry

Research has progressed into discerning the electrical and
chemical mechanisms relating to observed behaviors. It is
now known that specific hormones, neurotransmitters, or
other chemical substances controlled by the hypothalamus,
when manipulated, change behaviors. In economic
parlance, changes in hormones or neurotransmitters
change preference structures. Commonly studied economic
phenomena, such as addiction, and satiation have
footprints in blood samples and brain chemicals. With
neurotransmitters and hypothalmic hormones under its

control, the hypothalamus directly effects other parts of the body, and most especially the pituitary gland which alters, as an endocrine gland, the release of hormones, including the growth hormone.

The complexity of neurotransmitters and hormones makes present-day knowledge of their precise relationship to hypothalmic activities and behaviors the subject of advanced study. The pioneers who linked hypothalmic processes and chemical secretions largely came from the field of pharmacology: Gottlieb, Meyer, and Barbour. Gottlieb (1890) had found that certain drugs eliminated the heat effects resulting from piqûre fevers (research reconfirmed this finding seventy years later; see Wit and Wang, 1968). Meyer had the idea that warming or cooling hypothalmic regions might drive body temperatures in the opposite direction. The experiments of Barbour (1912) proved Meyer's conjecture to be true and Barbour was the first to interpret this area of the brain as the "human thermostat." From there, a rather steady stream of research attempted to better isolate regions and basic effects around this function.

The quest for the specific electrical pathways involved in this process came from Curt von Euler (1950), whose early research on *electrophysiology* preceded a flurry of similar experiments. The relationship between hypothalmic functions and electrical stimulation was finally accepted with the paper of Andersson et al. (1956) who used long-term implants without the use of anesthesia. As measurement and experimental techniques improved (e.g., gradient layer calorimetry and tympanic thermometry), various neurological pathways and firing patterns of hypothalmic neurons were discovered — i.e., firing rates of warm and cold receptors below and above a "set point."

Since the mid-1960s, a neurological explanation of how the human thermometer operates has been accepted. The chemical explanation for this process was started in the 1950s by biochemists who spent great efforts on understanding the role chemical substances (e.g., monoamines) that make this process work in a rather complex manner (given the multivariate nature of the energy balance equation); see early reviews in Benzinger (1977), Ito et al. (1972), Hellon (1975), Meyers (1977), Hochachka and Somero (1984), and Bligh and Voigt (1990) for recent advances. By the mid-1970s, a number of hormones and neurotransmitters (e.g., serotonin — 5-HT, norepinephrine) were found to be associated with this process. Hormonal variations associated with the metabolic rate, in particular, include catecholamines (norepinephrine and epinephrine), thyroxin (thyroid hormones), to a lesser extent testosterone, and the growth hormone, which can be associated with from 5 to 100 percent changes in metabolic functions in either the very short run, or over a period of weeks, depending on the hormone involved (Rhoades and Pflanzer 1996, p. 808).

A growing literature shows that homeostatic equilibrium is related to virtually all body fluids and functions that may or may not be directly related to thermoregulatory processes, but nevertheless guarantee the integrity of the organism (see, for example, Brenner and Stein 1987). Homeostatic processes have been demonstrated in psychiatry (Powles 1992), neurology (Vranic et al. 1991, and Blessing 1997), and general human biology (Chiras 1999). In other fields, substantial research continues to focus on limit conditions of the organism under severe stress (e.g., military and sports medicine), but also how these mechanisms affect or are affected by psychological processes (Folinsbee et al. 1978). Research started in the 1960s hoping to illuminate all hypothalmic effects and workings at the cellular, chemical, and electrical levels for humans will carry us over into the twenty-first century.

The Hypothalamus and Behavior

A number of authors have reviewed the relationship among the hypothalamus, hormones, neurotransmitters, and behavior (see, for example, Morgane and Panksepp 1980, Bloom et al. 1985, Donovan 1985, Brown 1994). For more general reviews of the limbic system and behavior, the reader is referred to the works cited above and to Mogenson et al. (1980), and Panskepp (1998) in particular. With the caveat that this is an emerging area, research has made fascinating progress in linking chemical secretions controlled by the hypothalamus (hormones, neurotransmitters, and other chemical substances), and homeostasis in general, to individual and social behaviors. The thermoregulatory role of the hypothalamus is but one of its many functions. Some of this understanding comes from research sponsored by the United States, Japanese, British, and Russian military services. The goal of these experiments is to understand physiological changes to the human organism under varying degrees of physiological stress but also to obtain the optimal food rations and living conditions for troops stationed or called to duty in different parts of the world.[2] These and other studies have found a direct link among conduction, convection, evaporation, and radiation on optimal clothing, food intake, housing, and workplace requirements (artificial air conditioning, heating, external appearance, insulation, etc.). Experimental animal research has shown, for example, that a change to hypothalmic functions can so fundamentally change a subject's preferences for food that it will starve to death in the face of free and unlimited food supply. Less radical experiments have demonstrated effects on appetite, body weight, mood, and comfort. The next chapter turns attention to direct thermoregulatory preference structures.

Metabolic functions aside, the anterior and preoptic hypothalmic areas are now known to control the gonads and sexual activity; hypothalmic neurons secret gonadoptropic-releasing hormones starting sometime in puberty. They also affect emotions, psychological balance, and social aggressivity. From animal research, good examples come from experiments conducted on crustaceans at Harvard Medical School's Department of Neurobiology. Lobsters have few but very large neurons, some visible to the human eye. This happenstance of nature makes them wonderful subjects when evaluating the effects of neurotransmitters on social behaviors. Edward Kravitz and his fellow researchers have considered the effects the neurotransmitter—hormone serotonin and norepinephrine (octopamine in lobsters) on social behavior, especially aggressivity. The research, including the injection of Prozac, indicates a strong relationship between these chemicals and aggressive, or social behavior.

There are direct parallels in psychiatry and psychology vis-à-vis the utility for certain products or services by humans. In the early 1980s, psychiatrists noted a strong relationship between exposure to sunlight and seasonal affective disorder (SAD), which in severe cases has lead to suicide or suicide ideation in patients. The hypothalamus is located adjacent to the optic chaism in humans and has been shown to be affected (electro-chemically stimulated) by the arrival of photons on the retina.

Beginning around 1990, phototherapy became recognized as a medical treatment of SAD and depression in countries near the poles, which historically have been known to have higher than average suicide rates. The reason is not bad weather, per say, but a chemical imbalance brought on by the lower inclination of the sun and the lower photon arrivals on the retina during long winter periods. Residents of countries on the other side of the equator experience similar effects, but with a six month lag, and residents of equatorial countries appear to be unaffected by SAD. Although highly controversial at first, the review in Parker

(1995, p. 83−113 and p. 161−168) lists some 134 studies linking suicide to solar climate and 340 studies showing a relationship between phototherapy, or solar activity, and seasonal affective disorder. This research has now isolated certain neurotransmitters that can, if consumed in synthetic derivative form (e.g., Prozac), have effects similar to phototherapy. While these effects on consumption are non-thermal, we will give some attention to psychological homeostasis, as this may vary by latitude. Otherwise, thermal homeostasis is given more emphasis here.

From Homeostasis to Economic Behavior

Establishing that homeostasis affects economic variances across countries requires two key concepts. The first is the observation that man is a species of tropical mammal. The second is the idea that there is a limited degree to which human autonomic physiological mechanisms can adjust to nontropical conditions. At some point, economic behavioral responses are required to achieve homeostasis, or *comfort*. Understanding the effects of latitudinal seasonalities is especially important.

"Man Is a Tropical Animal"

The above quote, coined by the distinguished biologist Peter Scholander, is quite meaningful here. Another way of stating it is "all humans are Equatorial Africans." From an evolutionary perspective, the anthropological record demonstrates that human ancestors originated in what was then the hot, perhaps dry, tropical savanna of East Africa. Only after about a million years did our ancestors, Homo Erectus, migrate to areas outside of this zone (about 500,000 years ago), but even then they spread mostly to the warmer areas of Asia and Europe. Only very recently, about 60,000 years ago, did man spread to the colder and darker temperate climes in significant numbers and reside there as permanent residents (coinciding with a major technological breakthrough — the controlled use of fire's radiant heat).

Clark and Edholm (1985, p. 134) provide a zoological explanation of Scholander's conclusion:

> Man is extremely well endowed with sweat glands and has more than any other mammal; because of the ability to sweat at a high rate man can maintain body temperature in hot climates without difficulty. There is a price to pay, requiring the replacement of the water and salt lost, but in many cases this is not a serious problem. Man is also almost hairless; this is not necessarily a great advantage in any climate but it is less of a disadvantage in hot climates than in cool or cold regions. Certainly for a highly sweating animal, a thick fur coat would be incompatible. If man were to live naked and maintain a body temperature close to 37°C he must have a climate where the temperature is of the order of 28 — 30°C. Otherwise, he has to have artificial means of insulation from the environment or suffer the discomforts and

> physiological costs of increasing heat production
> by shivering, or by active muscular movements. ...
> Another characteristic, which has already been
> mentioned, is that the metabolic rate of man in the
> resting nude state begins to rise when the
> environmental temperature drops below about
> 28°C; this is comparable with findings for other
> tropical animals.

The authors continue by summarizing research on how
tropical adaptation differs from that of animal residents of
cold areas (p. 134–135):

> [Scholander] examines the metabolic response of
> animals to cold and showed that the most
> important feature was the degree of insulation
> provided by fur. Animals adapted for life in sub-
> arctic conditions had such a thick coating of fur
> that they could not only withstand very cold
> conditions but could do so without increasing their
> metabolic rate. The critical temperature for such
> animals could be as low as -40°C as in the case of
> the arctic fox. Scholander measured the sub-
> clothing temperature of the Eskimo living in
> temperatures down to -40°C and showed that it
> was virtually the same as in men living in
> temperate or even warm environments. He
> claimed that the Eskimo is not so much adapted to
> cold, but he has contrived his environment to
> maintain a tropical climate beneath his clothing. . .

> Over a period of a year in the Antarctic the average
> sub-clothing temperature was approximately 33°C
> and similar to that recorded in people living in a
> temperate climate. This is approximately equiva-
> lent to a mean skin temperature of 34°C which is
> the usual level measured in conditions of thermal
> comfort.

Being tropical mammals, humans have but two responses
to temperature changes: autonomic or behavioral.
Autonomic processes (sweating, shivering, metabolism,
acclimatization) are somewhat flexible in humans, as with
other tropical animals, which allows one to survive in a
variety of climatic conditions, especially in the short run.
As shown in the previous chapter (figure 3.1), minimal
physiological effort is required in temperatures ranging
between 28°C and 30°C.

After certain limits are reached, however, humans resort to
behavioral responses. These vary from simple gestures
(e.g., rubbing one's arms after cold sensation, signaled by
the hypothalamus) to ingenious artificial methods, much of
which is reflected in certain technology and consumer
behaviors.

Adaptation

The diffusion of man geographically has occurred in a
nongenetic though similar fashion to the way other animal
species undergo what biologists and zoologists call

"adaptive radiation" or, in some disciplines, "divergent evolution." As an original population grows in size from its geographic center, it will eventually spread from its origin to exploit new habitats and food sources. Over time, geographically dispersed populations will adapt to the habitats encountered. In the long run, the separated populations will sufficiently evolve to become different species. Commonly cited examples of this process include the Australian marsupials that adapted into species of carnivores, herbivores, burrowers and fliers. On a smaller scale, Darwin (1859) observed the adaptive radiation of Finches in the Galapagos as evidence for his theory of evolution.

The mechanism at work in compliance with conservation laws (the hypothalamus) is genetically the same across all humans (being the most primitive part of the brain), and it is remarkably similar in its functions across various mammal species. Racial and other genetic variations observed in humans are literally, for homeostatic utility, only skin deep. Some species adapt to changes in their environs by migration. Others build structures that work locally (termite hills, beaver huts, etc.). The genius unique to humans is their ability to create a "comfortable" or "tropical" environment wherever they reside with only minor physiological adjustments. The costs or energy required in doing so, however, can not be equivalent everywhere (from the first law of thermodynamics). This is easy to see when considering the extremes. We have been able to send people to the moon and live under the Arctic

Ocean's ice cap in submarines. The farther the environment deviates from our tropically evolved set point, the laws of physics require that more compensation be made to a thermally comfortable zone. If immediate surroundings cannot supply what is necessary to obtain comfort (e.g., seal skins), humans have either migrated or invented consumable "products." Thus, space ships or submarines can be seen as very expensive climate chambers, while space suits and diving suits can be seen as very expensive clothes, all of which are most useful in climates which greatly deviate from the tropical set point.

Autonomic Limits: The Frontier of Physioeconomic Behavior

To understand invention and technology driven by homeostasis, one needs to consider the point at which autonomic responses are insufficient to provide comfort. The energy balance equation 3.5 has been directly translated to optimal consumption patterns of oxygen, food, clothing, housing, and energy by environmental physiologists. This has be done via experiment, measured voluntary intake, and revealed preferences of human and animal subjects. With thermoregulation, explaining observed variances requires further precision on the concept of thermal comfort, which is achieved when the body is in thermal neutrality.

All other factors being held constant, the thermal neutrality for a naked male human at rest is attained at $28-30^{\circ}$C within a homogenous atmosphere where the subject is acclimated (Houdas and Ring, p. 108—110). In this situation, the body is in thermal steady state without active thermoregulation (sweating or shivering). Heat produced at the basal metabolic rate equals the amount absorbed by the environs and the subject is comfortable. In this environment, the body stabilizes to a core homeostatic temperature of 37°C. In normal living conditions with relatively low humidity, the physiologically comfortable temperature range becomes affected by the fact that people tend to wear cloths, are somewhat mobile during the day, and are therefore not fully at rest. Under such conditions, thermal neutrality is achieved in practice at 22—24°C or 72—75°F (Houdas and Ring, p. 110). This range of thermal neutrality varies from one environment to another based on atmospheric conditions, adaptation, and acclimatization.

Adaptation is defined in Stanier et al. (p. 87) as "a feature of a species or of an individual animal—structural, physiological, or behavioral—which allows it to survive and reproduce under apparently adverse conditions, or when conditions change, or when the animal itself moves from one set of conditions to another." Acclimatization is defined as (p. 87) "a particular form of adaptation which allows survival in adverse or varying climatic conditions." After basic survival has been achieved, humans then strive for comfort. Thermal comfort is typically defined as "that condition of mind which expresses satisfaction with the thermal environment" (Fanger 1977, p. 145).

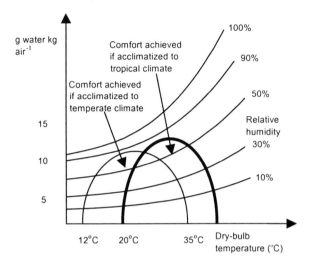

Figure 4.1
Thermal comfort for residents across climates (adapted from Stanier et al., 1994, p. 96)

In the absence of behavioral adaptation, thermal comfort depends on acclimatization. Figure 4.1, adapted from Stanier et al. (p. 96, who adapt from Folk 1974), shows the comfortable temperature ranges for various combinations of temperature, and relative humidity for residents acclimatized to tropical climates and temperate climates. For both climates, the ranges of thermal comfort increases with lower relative humidity. The average at low humidity is 23°C for temperate climates and 28°C for tropical climates.

As humidity rises, the ranges of temperatures narrow. In persons acclimatized to temperate climates, a relative humidity above 50 percent at temperatures over 25°C is not tolerable. For persons acclimatized to tropical climates, a relative humidity at 50 percent can be tolerated to temperatures of 30°C without discomfort. Similarly, tropical residents find temperatures below 18°C uncomfortable at any level of humidity, whereas residents of temperate climates find temperatures below 12°C uncomfortable. At high levels of humidity (e.g., 70 percent), tropical residents can feel comfortable at temperatures up to 25°C, whereas temperate residents find this level of humidity comfortable at 18°C. Between tropical and temperate acclimatization, there is a continuum for all climatic regions. For residents of regions with extreme conditions, the general trend continues, with rain forest residents feeling comfortable at the highest levels of humidity-temperature and residents above the Arctic Circle (irrespective or racial origin), feeling comfortable at the lowest ranges of temperature.

Strongly Seasonal Climates and Homeostasis

Environmental physiologists often reduce to the world to four climatic types that allow habitation for birds and mammals: (1) temperate, (2) arctic and subarctic, (3) dry tropical, and (4) wet tropical. Other regions prove too inhospitable for most species (i.e., extremely high altitudes or barren deserts in either high or low latitudes). If the discussion of thermal comfort is coupled with that of climate, studies have revealed that there are some places in the world where the citizens must adapt to multiple climatic conditions (discussed in chapter 6) to avoid discomfort (homeostatic disutility).

Climatically, some regions of the world have nearly tropical summers and freezing or in some cases Siberian winters (e.g., most of the U.S. east of the Rocky Mountain range). In these regions, residents never fully acclimatize to their climate and must consume both heating and air conditioning to achieve comfort. Others experience mild summers and very cold winters (e.g., Scandinavia) and have less difficulty adapting to the summer months (i.e., will have lower use for air conditioners). Still others have warm summers and mild winters (North Africa) and can afford low consumption of internal heating. The tropics generally have constant warm temperatures. Biologists point out that humans have genetically evolved to be at maximal physiological comfort in a warm locale (around 23°C) with a relative humidity approaching around 50 percent and an air movement of about 0.2m/s (Clark and Edholm 1985, p. 176). Very few places outside of the tropics have these prevailing conditions all year round, so humans like all other species, have adapted to (as opposed to conquered) temperate climates. It turns out that those who have to adapt the most (i.e., those who can not rely on purely autonomic mechanisms) are those living farthest from the tropics with the greatest seasonal variations.

Summary

Independent of race, creed, or culture, the human body has genetically evolved to be at greatest comfort in a warm climate at a relatively moderate level of humidity. It may also be true that the greatest psychological comfort is achieved in regions having a sufficiently high level of natural sunlight; again, near the equator. In response to cold, autonomic processes, including acclimatization, are used by the body to achieve comfort at different levels of temperature and humidity. As temperature and humidity are the primary sources of climatic variation in the world, one would expect worldwide differences in human strategies to achieve comfort. At differing points of temperature and humidity, autonomic processes hit their limits and active adaptation is required to maintain comfort or homeostasis. This process is invariably triggered by the hypothalamus which continually monitors internal and external stimuli and can react with quick and predictable precision. For thermoregulation, autonomic processes fail to achieve comfort when average temperatures (at any level of humidity) begin to fall below the 20°C to 25°C range, even for persons acclimatized to the world's coldest regions. In response to lower levels of sunlight, unlike adaptations to cold, humans residing nearer the poles have recently resorted to the consumption of artificial natural light, chemical substances and, perhaps, tourism.

A large number of researchers have dedicated their lives to understanding the workings of human limits. Research would have been stymied had it not been for the experimental method and, especially, the subjects. Heinz Gartmann (1957) in *Man Unlimited* offers tribute to human subjects. He details the travails of men and women who risked life and limb to reach human limits. "How far can humans free-fall without being subject to physical injury?" is but one of many limits that have lead to fascinating records but also tragic results. Basic physical concepts, or laws, brought to light by Newton and others who followed can now explain virtually all of these limits.

Recently, microeconomics has turned an eye toward experimental approaches common in the natural sciences (Hagel and Roth 1995). *The Economist* commented on what many feel is the raison d'être of these pursuits (May 8, 1999, p. 84):

> ...unlike physics, economics yields no natural laws or universal constants. That is what makes decisive falsification in economics so difficult. And that is why, without experiments, economics is not and never can be a proper science.

The next chapter demonstrates that neurological and physiological mechanisms, as affected by physics, certainly have an impact on fundamental economic behaviors. In this respect, experiments in the natural sciences may have already given economics a leg-up in the pursuit of general laws or constants.

Notes

1. See also Mercer (1989), Mackowiat et al. (1992), and Robertshaw (1974, 1977, 1979) for reviews.

2. Beyond what is covered in chapter 6, the interested reader can review these by searching the NTIS CD-Rom database, or Medline.

5 Homeostatic Preferences

No person who examines and reflects can avoid seeing that there is but one race of people on earth, who differ from each other only according to the soil and the climate in which they live.

—J.G. Stedman

The two previous chapters laid out the laws of energy conservation as they are known today and as they apply to humans. They further described the relationship between human physiological mechanisms and those laws. Based on these laws, one finds that the body strives for homeostasis or comfort (e.g., thermoregulation, psychological balance). This notion closely coincides with Jeremy Bentham's belief that humans ultimately maximize utility by pursuing pleasure while avoiding pain, both of which are fundamentally biological and psychological constructs. Humans are thus motivated via chemical processes regulated mostly by hypothalmic activity in response to external and internal stimuli. Whether hypothalmic in nature, or regulated elsewhere, homeostatic processes all have in common a "set point" around which consumption equilibrium converges. This chapter translates homeostasis to the utility domain for certain classes of goods and services. It is convenient here to call these "homeostatic goods."

Utility Functions — Are There Laws?

Utility functions are at the heart of economic analysis – a necessary condition for the discipline itself. If one began a discussion with "assume an economy devoid of utility for goods and services" it would be difficult to imagine the role of firms, an individual's motivation to work, or a need for political economy. Income, broadly defined, is endogenous to notions of utility, satisfaction, or happiness. Even if monetary income were absent, utility theory alone explains a vast number of economic behaviors whenever there is choice among alternatives.

Little is known about how preference structures and utility functions might vary from one country to the next. Traditionally it is assumed that there are no cross-national variations in utility. While Sen (1977), among others, has called for a utility-based notion of welfare, which can conceivably vary from person to person, or culture to culture, Silberberg (1978, p. 217–8) highlights the difficulties implied by this possibility:

> The assertion that consumers possess utility functions is a statement that people do in fact have preferences. How these preferences come to be, and why they might differ among people of different countries or ethnic groups, is a discipline

outside of economics. These are certainly interesting questions. They are also exceedingly difficult to grapple with.

Indeed, causal models or rigorous theories of utility creation and variation are few. Frequently, one arrives at cultural explanations, as in Becker (1998, p. 16 – 17):

> Culture exercises a sizable influence over preferences and individual behavior, whereas behavior has only a slow return influence on culture. Differences in culture cause considerable differences in preferences over goods, as with the taboo against eating pork among religious Jews and Moslems, or the tradition of filial obedience in Chinese and some other cultures. The economists' traditional assumption of "given" and stable preferences over goods seems to be much more consistent with the influence of culture on preferences than with the influence of personal capital and other kinds of social capital.

The primary difficulty in using culture as an explanatory variable is the lack of general theoretical appeal or fundamental principles. In addition to not identifying drivers of culture, such theories might easily use up all of the degrees of freedom by claiming that each country or culture has a unique heritage that makes utility functions specific to each.

Homeostatic Utility

This chapter now considers the utility for goods purchased in pursuit of homeostasis or comfort, as imposed by natural laws. Such utilities cut across all definitions of consumer groups, including national, ethnic, or cultural. For homeostatic goods, the relationships discussed in the previous chapter permit one to foresee (1) the shape of utility functions, (2) the direction of utility changes at any level of consumption, (3) the absolute magnitude limits to equilibrium consumption levels, (4) the types or bundles of aggregate goods and services consumed (given choice possibilities), and (5) the dynamics and variations of equilibrium patterns across countries.

Homeostasis can be defined as the maintenance of a body's constant state, within narrow limits, by a dynamic equilibrium.[1] Thermoregulation is but one example of homeostasis in physiology that humans must achieve. Others include homeostasis of body water, pH, ionic equilibrium, blood pressure, and body weight. From these physiological equilibria and the behavior implied by equation 3.5 (the law of conservation), one now knows that certain instantaneous and life-long utility curves must be of a particular functional form. The aggregate model one obeys is partially compensatory, meaning that one variable can be used as a substitute for any other, up to a point— overall homeostasis is always strived for. In the extremes, too much or too little consumption of any one or combinations of homeostatic goods can accelerate entropy to a point where utility vanishes. Physiologists do not view deviations from the set point as a "disutility," rather, they use terms such as discomfort, depression, deprivation, illness, and, if far enough, death (e.g., by intoxication, suicide, or failure of vital functions).

Figure 5.1 illustrates a homeostatic utility curve consistent with the laws outlined in the two previous chapters. In that figure, X is defined as the per capita consumption level of any homeostatic good and $U(X)$ as the satisfaction or utility (comfort in physiology; affect or mood in psychology) derived from that consumption level. If one is to stay true to physiology, consumption at a minimum must affect either internal or external receptors (e.g., including the five senses). In physiology, consumption is often seen as a combination of time and quantity (e.g., a "dose" or exposure to, say, a good for a given about of time). Here, consumption is defined in the literal sense and does not include "ownership" or "storing" that might be used for later consumption, arbitrage, or savings. For goods, such as paintings, that can be both consumed and represent a form of savings, the following applies to the part that is consumption (i.e., hours per day "enjoying" or "thinking about" the painting).

The shape of this utility curve is familiar to mathematicians, biologist, engineers, or others who study catastrophe theory, pioneered by René Thom. The function itself can be expressed mathematically in a variety of ways; its generic form is sometimes called a "catastrophic failure

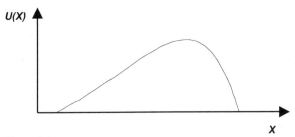

Figure 5.1
Homeostatic utility

curve" that has found general applicability to systems undergoing some form of external stress.[2] Utility increases in X to a certain level after which it *must* decay (sometimes called the slew). In humans, for example, any activity that tends to change core body temperature above 40°C or below 35°C generates this extreme relationship (as detailed in the previous chapter).

How does this function match up with neoclassical counterparts? The functional form itself does not contradict rational decision making. As long as constrained consumers maximize this function, they are rational. With a few exceptions, neoclassical utility functions exhibit nonsatiation, substitution, and decreasing marginals. Utility is assumed such that $U'(X)>0$ and $U''(X)<0$ for all levels in X; utility increases with greater levels of consumption, but at a diminishing rate. The assumptions are defended on the belief that "To deny these postulates is to assert strange behavior" (Silberberg, p. 221). Homeostasis is at odds with this view. For a large class of goods or behaviors, these assumptions violate certain laws of physics. They would do so even for nonhuman mammals whose existence relies solely on hunting or gathering. Homeostatic utility curves impose satiation, low or zero levels of substitution across certain goods (e.g., one cannot infinitely substitute clothing for food as these eventually become complements for persons in cold countries), and marginals must reach zero at some point, and then become negative after supersatiation.

The neoclassical function is generally sufficient to explain microeconomic behaviors since the interest here lies mostly in the region prior to the decline in utility. This decline, however, will not occur at the same level of consumption across all countries; hence its importance to macro-economics. This basic violation of the neoclassical tradition aside, it is apparent that one can apply most neoclassical concepts to homeostatic utility, though rationality leads to interior solutions.

Intuition

To defend this functional form, one can supplement *the laws* described in chapter 3 by appealing to intuition. Think of the consumption of any food item at a single sitting (or over the life span of the individual). One gram of sugar consumption derives utility, but if not sufficient in quantity, the body physically suffers. At some point, however, the organism is saturated. Consumption beyond this point leads to a catastrophic failure (disutility) and, potentially, death (zero utility forever). The listing in table 5.1 summarizes for a variety of nutrients the implications for deviations around the upper and lower crisis points for humans. To remain between these two points, nutritionists typically calculate recommended daily intakes (adapted from McArdle et al. 1991, p. 51).[3]

In practice, one rarely reaches the point of excess, as the brain signals physiological intoxication or stress. In some cases, the hypothalamus shuts off many motivational centers at once, inducing one to faint or sleep, thus allowing the body to concentrate on recovery. Typically, well before the fainting point, one responds to changes in neurotransmitters and/or hormones (i.e., one "feels bad"); consumption is autonomically halted. Carpenter (1996, p. 288) notes that one tends to be relatively unconscious of these mechanisms or motivations, while "even the most complex mental processes can sometimes be carried out without being conscious of the fact at all."

Homeostatic utility appeals to intuition for all things affecting human sensation or physiology (food, clothing, internal heating, etc.), but it also relates to many forms of psychological consumption as these are bounded by certain physiological considerations (which are in turn constrained by physical laws). One will, for example, eventually face a

Table 5.1
Effects of deficient or excess consumption of certain nutrients

Substance	Signs of deficiency	Signs of excess
Calcium	Rickets, stunted growth, osteoporosis	Not reported
Phosphorus	Convulsions	Erosion of jaw
Sodium	Cramps, apathy	High blood pressure
Iron	Anemia	Siderosis, cirrhosis of liver
Fluorine	Tooth decay	Neurologic disturbance, tooth mottling
Zinc	Growth failure, small sex glands	Fever, nausea, vomiting, diarrhea
Copper	Anemia	Wilson's disease
Selenium	Anemia	Gastrointestinal disorders, lung irritation
Iodine	Goiter	Depressed thyroid activity
Molybdenum	Not reported	Inhibition of enzymes
Chromium	Impaired ability to metabolize glucose	Skin and kidney damage
Oxygen	Suffocation	Convulsions
Calories	Wasting	Obesity
Water	Thirst, dehydration	Headache, nausea, edema, high blood pressure

choice between sleep and ever increasing levels of any quality-specific entertainment at a single sitting, or over the life span of the individual (e.g., looking at, or thinking about a painting). For higher quality-specific quantities, the laws of nature dictate, via hypothalmic rhythms and resulting hormones and neurotransmitters, that one will eventually prefer and then consume sleep. Indeed, since all forms of consumption are bounded by time, there will always be homeostatic utility. As Becker (1993, p. 386) notes "economic and medical progress have greatly increased length of life, but not the physical flow of time itself, which always restricts everyone to 24 hours per day. So while goods and services have expanded enormously in rich countries, the total time available to consume has not." Within those 24 hours, we are obligated to dedicate some 30 to 50 percent of our time to eating, sleeping, and fulfilling basic biological functions. All other forms of consumption that require time, including entertainment, therefore, become homeostatic. To avoid a list of ad hoc examples, it is useful to return to the discussion of how physical laws translate to preferences.

Homeostatic Preferences

Figure 5.2 shows homeostatic indifference curves implied by figure 5.1 for a consumer considering consumption bundles of two goods, X_1 and X_2. In the top figure, the curves are drawn in a rather continuous manner since the two goods are substitutes (two types of food supplying carbohydrates). Consumption will likely occur on the

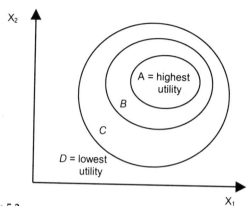

Figure 5.2
Homeostatic preferences: substitutes

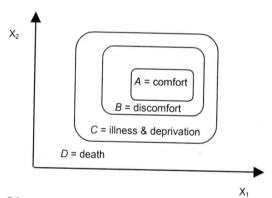

Figure 5.3
Homeostatic preferences: quasi-complements

southwest quadrant of each indifference contour (assuming higher total cost to consume the more one consumes). In the bottom figure, the goods become complements (food versus indoor heating); again, not consuming enough or too much of either good causes disutility. In both figures, one can consider broad zones of consumption bundles, labeled A, B, C, D. One sees that $U(D)<U(C)<U(B)<U(A)$. Consider, for example, food consumption; then D would represent death (via starvation or intoxication), C would indicate illness, B discomfort, and A comfort. The narrow range of consumption that allows comfort is consistent with homeostasis, though the shapes of these contours can be drawn in a variety of ways, depending on the goods being considered (e.g., shaped as crescents).

Dynamics

Homeostatic preferences are consistent with the neurophysiological notion of "motivational gradients." Based on a given perceived need, these gradients instruct the body, like the yellow pages, where to go. While these gradients or "motivational maps" are believed to be embodied in the hippocampus (Carpenter, p. 273–274), it is "the hypothalamus, as a center to which autonomic afferents project, and which itself monitors such physiological states of the blood as glucose concentration, temperature and osmolarity, as well as circulating hormones, that defines one's state of need. It is also in the hypothalamus that primary consummatory responses such as eating and drinking may be triggered off by electrical stimulation"(p. 275). The dynamic monitoring of "need" drives consumption to the steady state. "Tropistic gradients", in biology, closely resemble homeostatic indifference contours, or motivational gradients. Tropistic growth is defined as the directional growth of, for example, a plant organ (root, limb) in response to an external stimulus, such as light, water, gravity, touch/friction, or free air. Growing toward a stimulus is called a positive tropism whereas growth away from the stimulus is a negative tropism. Geotropisms consider the effects of gravity; similarly for hydrotropism (water), phototropism (light), and thigmotropism (physical contact). Tropisms are regulated by internal and external mechanisms. For a plant, the motivation to choose a growth path may be long-run survival and/or competition for scarce resources. Irrespective of starting position, the steady-state growth path is toward-away from a set point determined by the stimulus.

Figures 5.2 and 5.3, in this case, might be considered maps of motivational tropism with all behaviors converging to a point falling within zone A, irrespective of the starting position in B or C. If one is currently consuming at a level greater than that found comfortable for both goods, then consuming less of either product increases utility and one approaches the steady state. If this zone systematically varies from one country to another, in absolute terms, then two countries can have equal marginal comforts, but at different steady-state homeostatic consumption levels.

The intertemporal nature of homeostatic consumption has been extensively studied in biology and physiology (though not using the notion of utility). A textbook example is the consumption of air by the lungs—a homeostatic problem. The lung has a certain fixed capacity to breathe fresh air and exhale "used" air of a different chemical composition. The exchange between ambient air and the lungs respects a homeostasis of a specific chemical balance. The processes by which this is achieved is characterized by a linear updating function, where the concentration of the chemical in time t is C_t, and in $t+1$, C_{t+1}:

$$C_{t+1} = \alpha + \beta C_t \tag{5.1}$$

where α and β are constants that reflect the ambient chemical concentration times the fraction of air exchanged, and one minus the fraction of air exchanged with the environment, respectively (Adler 1998, p. 82). The steady-state equilibrium, C^*, is achieved via the updating process shown in figure 5.4. For all starting positions above C^*, the cobweb leads to a reduction over time in concentration (consumption); for all starting positions below C^*, concentrations increase (figure 5.5). Of course, the updating function itself can shift over time or vary from one person to the next (e.g., due to a person's age or gender). The interest here is whether this updating function will systematically vary from country to country (for the average citizen residing in each), thus resulting in different steady state consumption levels C^*.

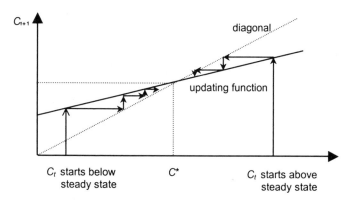

Figure 5.4
Homeostatic consumption dynamics

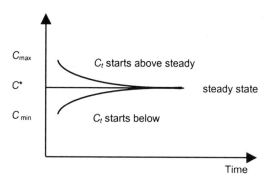

Figure 5.5
Homeostatic consumption steady state

Consumption Functions

The implications of the preference structures presented in figure 5.2 and the unconstrained consumption dynamics in figure 5.4 are far reaching, especially as these might interact with constraints in income or relative prices across goods. For homeostatic consumption, it can be easily shown that shifts in income or relative price changes lead to discontinuities in the form of absolute limits on Engle curves, offer curves, demand functions, and consumption functions. For example, all homeostatic goods become "quasi-inferior" in the limit, or have truncated Engle curves. The Slutsky equation and resulting demand and consumption functions also face truncation, or areas over which they are either not defined or are "flat." While these microeconomic implications are interesting, one is best served by focusing on aggregate consumption functions for homeostatic products.

Figure 5.6 shows, for example, the consumption function for homeostatic goods such as nutrients contained in food (e.g., calories, protein, or lipids). It has a positive intercept since zero consumption implies death. If all forms of mechanical work are included as income (hunter-gatherer income), the curve might be drawn through the origin.[4] As income (Y) rises, consumption hits an absolute plateau or limit (for a given good and consumer). This plateau can rise or fall not only based on a consumer's age, metabolic rate, etc., but also over time, seasons, or across countries.

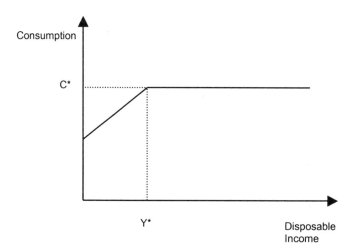

Figure 5.6
Homeostatic consumption functions

For most physiological consumption items, this plateau will always be observed in the very short-run and for some goods can be calculated externally (recommended daily requirements) using physiological concepts. The same plateau exists in the long-run if one considers the life-time consumption of the individual or household. Consuming homeostatic goods beyond the plateau, again, leads to discomfort, or eventually catastrophic failure. For those goods with explicit prices, income Y^* is required to attain maximum comfort consumption, C^*. The marginal propensity to consume beyond C^* is zero; the average propensity to consume at higher levels of income $(Y^* < Y)$ falls rapidly. Both of these conditions would be observable after consumption has reached its unconstrained steady state (i.e., at the point where income, or relative prices, no longer inhibit dynamics to the steady state).

If incomes are well beyond the point where C^* is reached, short-run policies designed to increase or decrease consumption-savings (e.g., changes in interest rates), will have little or no effect on homeostatic consumption. The more these represent a substantial part of overall consumption, and the more incomes surpass Y^* for these types of items, the less such policies can affect overall consumption. Consider a world where there are only consumers of oxygen—a free public good. No policy, in such a world, could alter the steady-state consumption level. Where oxygen is costly, and one is below the steady state, one would be chemically motivated to generate income to attain C^*. In this case, all other goods are complements to oxygen, so intertemporal shifts in consumption are limited.

Cross-Country Variations in the Steady State, C^*

The discontinuities implied by homeostatic preference structures and consumption dynamics are imposed by physics-based physiological and psychological limits of the human organism. Subsequent chapters will discuss how these preference structures and steady-state consumption levels must vary from one country to another, but in the long run will be similar across those with similar environmental conditions. As climatic regions are themselves spatially correlated in an asymmetric manner, so too will equilibrium consumption patterns for these goods. If prices are international, then the requisite income required to reach similar levels of physiological comfort will also vary across countries. Broadly, this discussion applies to various forms of food, clothing, housing, and energy. Other goods and services consumed in the pursuit of income to purchase homeostatic goods might also be effected by these variations (e.g., a certain fraction of education and transportation). Since direct homeostatic consumption (food, clothing, housing, and household energy), represents up to 50 percent of total consumption in developed countries, and up to 90 percent in low income countries, the focus will be mostly on these items.

Summary

Lacking explicit notions of utility, relative prices, and budget constraints, core texts on neurophysiology stop short of linking chemical homeostasis and economics. A few make casual remarks, however, on how these relationships must affect behavior. The following observation by Carpenter (1996, p. 274), a neuro-physiologist at Cambridge University, on the role of the hypothalamus is an example:

> Perhaps it is difficult for us to accept the notion that our own richly complex lives, with the apparent wealth of choices open to us, and our sense of liberty to choose among them, could possibly be determined by so simple a mechanism [the hypothalamus]. But as Herbert Simon (1981) has said, human behavior is really rather simple,

but because people live in very complex physical, man-made and social environments, their actual behavior appears extremely complicated; thus the path traced out by an ant moving over rough ground may be very complex in appearance, even though its behavior is simply directed at getting back to its nest. In fact, by averaging over a large number of individuals, it is not difficult to measure quite directly the same kinds of tropistic gradients for us humans that work so well in describing what an amoeba does.

The next chapter summarizes experimental, time series, and cross-sectional empirical evidence confirming that a large portion of economic consumption predictably varies across countries in the steady state. The "kinds of tropistic gradients" considered are generated from homeostatic utility functions discussed in this chapter. While focusing on physiological consumption, the next chapter also touches on psychological consumption, as this may be equally related to chemical homeostasis.

Notes

1.   Folk 1974, p. 88.

2.   For example, $U(X) = X^a e^{-x}$ or $U(X) = (a-X)e^X - a$, or similar functions, are commonly used.

3. A similar list can be constructed for vitamins and other nutrients (McArdle et al. 1991, p.46−47).

4. A baby's cry or a beggar's panhandling can be seen to represent mechanical work designed to increase food consumption.

6 Homeostatic Consumption

After food, clothing and lodging are the two great wants of mankind.

— Adam Smith[1]

Environmental physiologists, medical climatologists, and biophysicists have not shied from making explicit statements, after considerable study, on optimal or steady-state levels of consumption across a variety of goods and services.[2] The sixty years of field and laboratory research on which these statements are based have focused on establishing various limits to human comfort for numerous consumption items. Though psychological consumption has recently been considered (e.g., entertainment or products affecting mood and depression), the bulk of research has been conducted on food, clothing, housing, and medicine. Purely physiological studies consider changes in skin temperature and other physical changes to different environments, whereas applied research considers self-imposed temperature or material preferences by subjects in climate chambers or exposed to different material surroundings. From this literature, one now knows how the human body naturally prefers different materials and ambient temperature combinations consistent with the laws of thermodynamics and the workings of the hypothalamus.

Experimental Findings

It is difficult to do justice to this extensive literature; Parker (1995) provides an extensive bibliographic review of over 1,000 related studies.[3] Early studies of how humans adapt to thermal discomfort yielded a number of intriguing methodologies. Some considered matrices of basic human activities, for any given thermal situation, by experimentally manipulating temperature and other environmental factors in climate chambers. Garry et al. (1955) and Yoshimura and Weiner (1966), for example, separated an average human's day into some twenty basic activities and found preferred consumption during each activity under differing thermal conditions. Activities included bedmaking, cooking, dressing, running, sitting, sleeping, standing, and walking.

Studies of revealed preference typically place subjects in a climate chamber, who are residents acclimatized to particular parts of the globe, over either short or long periods of time and allow them to choose the temperature at which they feel comfortable via a thermostat. Subjects are dressed in a variety of clothing (from nude, to cotton underwear to space suits with the headgear removed), asked to perform various tasks (mental calculations, read, perform light work, exercise, etc.) and are monitored for various temperatures (e.g., skin, rectal), and body fluids (e.g., blood, urine, etc.). Experiments have also been performed for food consumption, housing and other behaviors testing preferred limits under homeostasis. Collections of these experiments dating from WWII to the present are reported in Yoshimura and Weiner (1966), Durand and Raynaud (1979), Robertshaw (1977, 1979), Hochachka and Somero (1984).

Revealed preference structures or reactions have been validated as existing for other animal species as well. These are typically exposed to various thermal conditions or physical substances replicating environmental effects; see the collections given in Durand and Raynaud (1979), Lomax and Schonbaum (1983, 1989), and Cooper et al. (1986). Military studies, available from the National Technical Information Service, also present volumes of experimental and field experiments relating to optimal consumption patterns for persons stationed in the different climatic zones of the world, or those involved in military- or space-related occupations, which often place workers under high levels of thermal stress.

In what follows, variations across latitudes will be considered as experienced by average human residents, though the same principles apply to other mammal species. A useful starting point is the left-hand side of the energy balance equation 3.5 which is mostly regulated by metabolic processes from food and oxygen consumption. From there, how housing and clothing consumption relate to the right-hand side will be discussed. Adam's Smith observance that after food, clothing and lodging are our two great wants, in fact, falls directly in line with the two sides of the equation.

Metabolism and Oxygen

Substantial research has been conducted on metabolism and food intake across ambient thermal conditions. Food preferences and intake functions are now understood to be controlled by specific brain processes involving tastes, olfactory stimuli, and other mechanisms mostly relating to the lateral hypothalamus (Rolls 1997). Most studies have been conducted on primates and pigs, but some have directly considered humans while controlling for a number of external factors, including income and sociocultural origin.

Figure 6.1 shows the relationship between thermal conditions and metabolic rates across a broad range of temperatures manipulated in climate chambers on subjects resting naked, adapted from Clark and Edholm (1985).[4] Metabolic rates remain fairly constant between 20°C and 30°C. In this range, the physiological demand for food and oxygen is at its lowest. Below 20°C, heat production increases in an exponential manner. This nonlinear pattern is also indicated in Blaxter (1989, p. 183) for oxygen consumption: the colder the temperature, the greater the consumption of oxygen. At higher temperatures, there is a wide range of temperatures where oxygen consump-

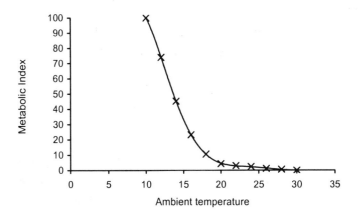

Figure 6.1
Metabolic rates and temperatures (adapted from Clark and Edholm, 1985, p. 155)

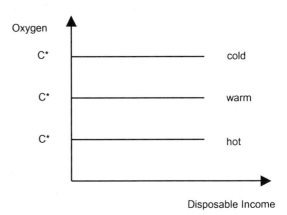

Figure 6.2
Consumption functions for oxygen across thermal conditions

tion is relatively constant. Consumption functions for oxygen are shown in figure 6.2. With no explicit price, due to its abundance, the steady-state marginal propensity to consume oxygen is zero everywhere, and the average propensity to consume falls. If oxygen was the only thing that humans consumed, there would be no utility derived from income or savings.

Oxygen, of course, is not the only thing humans consume, and we certainly do not live in climate chambers, resting naked. The consumption of food, clothing, and housing are responses to two basic problems: comfort and social norms. As these are not free goods, a complex interplay takes place whereby consumers must satisfy both physiological and social needs, while being constrained by the heat exchange equation discussed in chapter 3. Since food consumption can be partially offset by housing and clothing, it becomes difficult to isolate the effects of ambient temperature on each. In all cases, the laws of conservation acting on homeotherms requires that the combination of these maintain a 37°C internal core body temperature. One knows, therefore, that an exponential increase in consumption (in heat or metabolic equivalence) of one or a combination of these three items must occur below an ambient temperature of 20°C to avoid suffering for persons residing in the colder areas of the world, relative to the consumption levels of those residing toward the equator.

As clothing, food, and shelter are scarce and costly to acquire, as opposed to oxygen, there is a positive marginal propensity to consume for the physiological aspects of these goods up to C^*, or a physiological raison d'être for income up to Y^*. To understand the net effects on metabolism, studies of long-term residents of regions with different environmental conditions have difficulties controlling for things such as diet and infrastructure. Nevertheless, these indicate that persons residing in colder regions tend to have from 10 to 20 percent higher metabolic rates than residents of the tropics who are afforded adequate clothing and shelter (Rhoades and Tanner 1995). In other words, a certain percent of the variations shown in figure 6.1 is compensated for by a combination of food, clothing, and shelter. As will now be shown, the direction of consumption for each of these is the same—colder temperatures leads to higher steady-state consumption to achieve equivalence in homeostatic comfort, as dictated by the human tropical set point.

Food: Thermal Effects

The Food and Agriculture Organization (FAO) of the United Nations has long been concerned with understanding human nutrition requirements across countries. The effects of heat transfer have been an issue. In its *Handbook on Human Nutritional Requirements* (FAO, 1974, p. 11), the following is noted:

> That human beings eat less food in a hot climate than they do in a cold climate is generally recognized, but it is extremely difficult to express

the relationship between climate and food needs quantitatively.

Fundamentally, the difficulty lies in the fact that the right-hand side of the heat exchange equation 3.5 has multiple parameters: conduction, convection, evaporation, and radiation. Clothing and shelter thus relate to dietary preferences and controlling for these becomes problematic. For these reasons, the FAO has not used climate as an indication of caloric needs but rather has settled on looking at means and variances of local intake that may account for such differences implicitly (FAO 1996). As mentioned earlier, however, failure to consider such thermal effects may lead to erroneous standards.

The difficulty of measuring effects should not deter research in understanding and quantifying a known relationship. The fundamental question is: Would the average resident consume less food being acclimatized and appropriately or comfortably sheltered and dressed in a hot environment compared to the average resident acclimatized and comfortably sheltered and dressed in a cold climate? Ideally, the study would control for the individual tastes of the people, their cultural origins, income, and education levels.

Two broad sources of research have considered this precise question: scientific expeditions and military studies, reviewed more extensively in Parker (1995). In these, food, clothing, and shelter are fundamental to the success of missions. The variance of conditions faced by personnel stationed in high-altitude weather stations, polar observation settlements, or military bases, versus equatorial islands and all sorts of thermal conditions in between, virtually replicate the variations seen across known habitats or countries. In each case, the optimal combination of food, clothing, and shelter is desired, knowing that personnel and their families in the colder areas will only need, for example, heavy clothing for a few hours or less per day.

Folk et al. (1998) reports that residents living in the colder regions of the world, above 60° north latitude, number only approximately 208,000 (or .003 percent of the world's population). Their diets consist mostly of fish and sea mammals, with little vegetable matter. Polar expeditions whose members originate from temperate climates adjust their dietary preferences to those of native residents. Table 6.1, from Folk et al. (1998, p. 201), shows caloric intake for scientific missions to cold and temperate climates. Consistent with the observation that metabolism of residents in colder areas are higher than in warmer areas of the world, caloric intakes and concentrations of fat increase in the colder regions, despite high levels of protective clothing and shelter.

Studies conducted on U.S. military personnel stationed in bases for extended periods (e.g., over one year) indicate similar results. Figure 6.3 is adapted from Blaxter (1989, p.

Table 6.1
Average food intake preferences across temperatures

| Location | Caloric temp. °C | Intake | Caloric supply, % | | | Total |
			Proteins	Carbohydrates	Fats	
Churchill, Canada	-27	5235	12	46	42	100
Operation Muskox	-15	4400	13	45	42	100
Pacific Islands	26	3400	13	54	33	100
38th Div., Luzon	28	3200	13	54	33	100

Source: Adapted from Folk et al. (1998, p. 201, Table 5-6).

204–206) who notes that the caloric data reflect the fact that the military personnel were appropriately clothed and sheltered to protect them from their environments. The relationship between temperature and voluntary caloric intake is statistically significant and the cross-sectional explained variance is extremely high (R^2=.91). Whether the fact that food has lower digestibility in colder regions, or whether there are higher metabolic demands, the data reveal a net increase of voluntary food intake as outdoor temperature declines.

The fact that housing and clothing do not fully offset the effects of ambient temperature is consistent with experimental research showing that even limited amounts of time in the cold, or breathing cold air, results in metabolic changes. The hypothalamus, in this regard, is an extremely sensitive thermostat affecting appetite. Short of living in a "biosphere," persons residing in the colder regions of the world are more likely than not to voluntarily consume more food than had they been residents near the equator. Again, the data indicate that this result holds true irrespective of the population's ethnic or cultural origins. Similar studies have been conducted on other mammals (e.g., pigs), and they have found identical findings using climate chambers; see Parker (1995) for a list of some 100 related studies.

A telltale sign of this thermal effect on preferences can also be seen in the seasonal patterns of food consumption in countries where food prices and incomes are fairly stable (e.g., the eastern United States). In these places, highest carbohydrate, protein, and fat consumption levels are reached in the cold season and drop in the hottest season. This occurs, despite the residents having adequate shelter and clothing (see, for example, the studies in Parker, 1995, p. 196−204). This effect is quite different than seasonal consumption levels in countries with constant climates. In lesser developed countries, where food security is low and thermal seasonality is minimal, swings in consumption may reflect seasonal changes in income or prices and, thus, reflect physiological suffering. In many equatorial countries, seasons are marked by their levels of humidity which would have a smaller effect on voluntary food intake.

Food: Consumption Functions

If all persons were to achieve steady-state comfort from food consumption, C*(food) would be lowest in warmer areas of the world and higher in cooler areas (assuming adequate shelter and housing). This will be true at the intercept (0 income) and the plateau. If prices are international, the consumption functions in figure 6.4 reflect the aggregate physiological aspects of food across

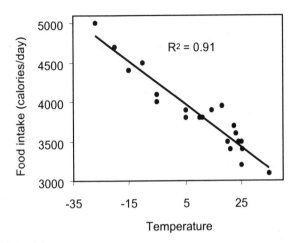

Figure 6.3
Voluntary food intake of military personnel stationed in different climates (adapted from Blaxter 1989, p. 205)

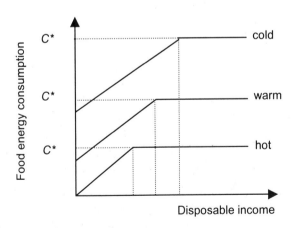

Figure 6.4
Consumption functions for homeostatic food energy across countries

countries with different thermal conditions. Although the slopes and magnitudes of these curves are purely illustrative, one sees that warm countries require less food (or income spent on food) than colder countries to achieve homeostatic comfort. Once comfort is achieved across all countries, the marginal propensity to consume food falls to zero everywhere and the average propensity to consume falls at higher levels of income.

Two interesting results derive from the idea that different countries might not share the same utility or consumption functions. First, the "over consumption" of food, or obesity, need not vary by ambient thermal condition. Second, as incomes surpass Y^*, there should be no correlation between income dynamics and aggregate food consumption dynamics.

Food: Obesity across Countries

Obesity is the excessive storage of energy in the tissues, beyond that required for physical comfort. According to figure 6.4, obesity can exist anywhere, but at different levels of caloric intake. One would expect, therefore, that caloric consumption varies by thermal situation, but not obesity. Figure 6.5 plots obesity prevalence against absolute latitude using data reported by the World Health Organization report on Obesity (WHO, 1998). The data reflect the year closest to 1990 reported, among adults with a body mass index over 30; virtually all of the data were

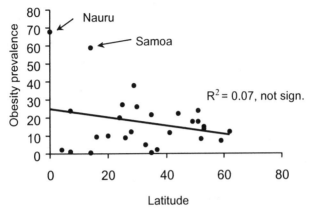

Figure 6.5
Prevalence of obesity and absolute latitude, 1990 or nearest; adapted from
WHO (1998, p. 22–35)

reported during the years 1989 to 1991. A similar
relationship is observed for men, women, and the average
across genders, which is plotted in figure 6.5 across the
thirty-one countries reported.

As indicated, there is no statistical relationship between
solar climate and obesity. Though the slope appears
negative, the R^2-statistic of 0.07 is not statistically
significant ($p\text{-}value < .15$), nor is the coefficient on latitude.
Concerning the two apparent outliers, Nauru and Samoa,
the WHO (p. 31) notes that "Polynesians seem leaner than
Caucasians at any given body size, and so the prevalence of
obesity in Polynesian populations may not be quite as high
as is currently estimated using Caucasian-derived
classifications based on BMI." If one takes out these two

outliers, the regression line falls flat and the R^2-statistic falls to .008 (not significant) confirming the lack of a relationship between latitude and obesity.

Food: Consumption Dynamics

Figure 6.4 also indicates that as incomes rise beyond a certain level, caloric intake hits an asymptote. Time series within a given country, therefore, will reveal that caloric intake remains fairly constant or is unrelated to income increases after a certain level of consumption (i.e., calories becomes quasi-inferior goods). Figures 6.6 and 6.7 plot caloric consumption across a sample of twenty-nine countries for which caloric intake data have been collected since the 1930s by the United Nations. Over the fifty-year span, average caloric intake has increased somewhat across the sample, though it appears to be reaching an asymptote of approximately 3,000 calories. The variance indicated in figure 6.8 indicates conditional convergence in these consumption levels, meaning that some countries appear to be converging to a relatively high steady state (near 3,000 calories in colder countries), while others are converging toward a lower level (near 2,000 calories in warmer countries). The simple correlation between caloric intake and latitude is .73 (*p-value*<.0001). Despite the substantial increases in incomes and life expectancies for many countries since W.W.II, caloric consumption for a large number of these has remained remarkably stable — supporting the notion of a homeostatic consumption plateau:

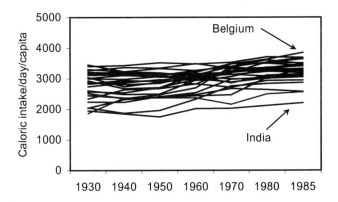

Figure 6.6
Caloric intake per capita: 1930–1985 (source: United Nations consumption surveys)

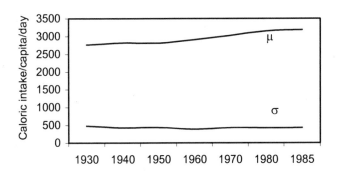

Figure 6.7
Mean and cross-country dispersion of caloric consumption per capita: 1930–1985

Country	1930	1985
Australia	3,300	3,326
Norway	3,210	3,219
Iceland	3,160	3,145
Sweden	3,120	3,049
Finland	3,000	3,080

The difficulties in collecting broad and complete household consumption time series data lead many empirical studies of caloric intake to focus on caloric supply. As might be expected for a mostly perishable good, consumption is highly correlated with supply, the dynamics of which closely track the consumption trends shown in figures 6.6 and 6.7. Figure 6.8 plots daily caloric supply, per capita, for a static sample of 147 countries from 1961 to 1994, as reported by the World Resources Institute (1999). Unlike the dynamics observed for income per capita over this same time period, which look more like a funnel, caloric consumption appears to look more like a tunnel; the divergence remaining fairly constant over the thirty-five year period. Figure 6.9 shows that the average caloric supply, μ, has increased somewhat since 1961, though is asymptotically approaching a value near 2,500 calories, and the dispersion, σ, appears to be reaching a steady state value of approximately 500. The point in time where the absolute range of supply was at its maximum occurred in the late 1970s when Cambodia was ruled by one of the more repressive regimes in modern history.

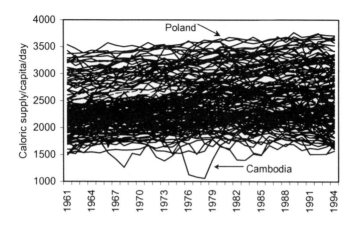

Figure 6.8
Supply of calories per capita per day (147 countries)

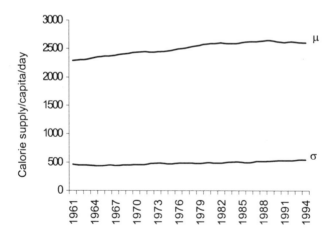

Figure 6.9
Worldwide mean and dispersion of caloric supply per capita
per day across 147 countries

In addition to calories, the human organism requires lipids and protein, which can be called upon for thermoregulation and maintaining the integrity of the organism. For these two nutrients, figures 6.10 and 6.11 for protein, and figures 6.12 and 6.13 for fat, all show consumption tunnels, as indicated for calories. The correlation to latitude for both protein and fat are of the expected sign and same magnitude for calories (p-values<.0001). Similar tunnels exist for other categories including milk, cereal, sugar, and potatoes.[5]

Food: Aggregation Issues

The effects of supply proximity certainly exist, especially as one disaggregates the consumption basket into individual items. Beer consumption per capita, for example, is 200 to 600 percent higher in Germany and Denmark, than it is in Mediterranean or southern European countries: Portugal, Greece, France, and Spain. Wine consumption per capita, however, is some 200 to 300 percent higher in these southern countries, compared to Germany and Denmark. The energy balance equation applies to larger aggregates and across varying thermal conditions. Testing Montesquieu's conjecture on alcohol requires looking at consumption aggregated across all product forms and over a sample of countries spanning equatorial and colder regions.

At the broadest level, for 1 gram of carbohydrates, the human body absorbs 4 Calories; for 1 gram of protein, the body absorbs 4 Calories; and for 1 gram of fat, the body absorbs 9 Calories. If one assumes that humans strive for a given homeostatic quantity of calories and cut back on, say, fat, one can anticipate

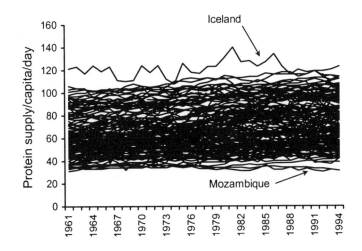

Figure 6.10
Protein supply per capita per day (grams)

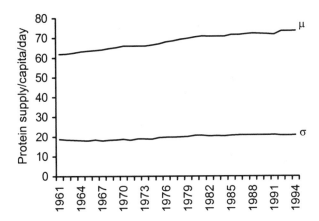

Figure 6.11
World mean and dispersion protein supply per capita per day
(grams)

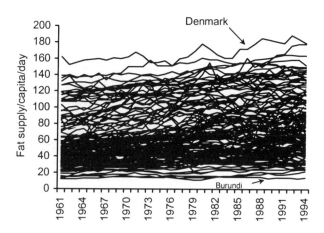

Figure 6.12
Fat supply per capita per day (grams) across 147 countries

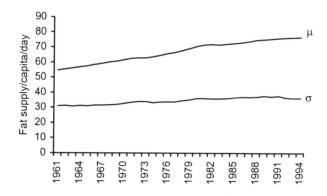

Figure 6.13
World mean and dispersion fat supply per capita per day (grams) across
147 countries

an increase in the consumption of either protein or carbohydrates, whichever the hypothalamus creates a craving for and/or whichever is economically available. Nutrition experts in the United States are currently divided on the ability of Americans to reduce caloric consumption. During the 1970s, Americans began shifting dietary patterns away from fats, from about 44 percent of caloric intake to approximately 34 percent by 1999.[6] This trend followed strong public recommendations to lower fat intake to reduce obesity and related illness. During that time, however, obesity rose by 50 percent as consumers shifted to high quantities of low-fat carbohydrates found in processed foods. Average U.S. residents, despite substantial improvements in clothing and housing over the decades, have yet to adopt a low-calorie diet.

Food: Economic Geography versus Physiology

To Adam Smith, food is "the greatest want of mankind," or the primary reason to expend work energy.[7] The following passages are representative of many that Smith devotes to food, especially how it relates to economic geography:

> Human food seems to be the only produce of land which always and necessarily affords some rent to the landlord. Other sorts of produce sometimes may, and sometimes may not, according to circumstances.[8]

> Food is, in this manner, not only the original source of rent, but every other part of the produce of land which afterwards affords rent, derives that part of its

value from the improvement of the powers of labor in producing food by means of the improvement and the cultivation of the land.[9]

To Smith, a well fed population then seeks other goods and land fulfills a second purpose:

The increasing abundance of food, in consequence of increasing improvement and cultivation, must necessarily increase the demand for every part of the produce of land which is not food and which can be applied either to use or to ornament.[10]

The demand for "ornamental" goods or nonnecessities, therefore, is indirectly generated from food demand, homeostatic satiation, and residual profits from cultivation:

Whatever increases the fertility of land in producing food, increases not only the value of the lands upon which the improvement is bestowed, but contributes likewise to increase that of many other lands, by creating a demand for their produce. The abundance of food, of which, in consequence of the improvement of land, many people have the disposal beyond what they themselves can consume, is the great cause of the demand both for the precious metals and the precious stones, as well as for every other conveniency and ornament of dress, lodging, household furniture and equipage.[11]

Smith thus argues that land becomes the source of population, labor, and wages:

> Countries are populous, not in proportion to the number of people whom their produce can clothe and lodge, but in proportion to that of those whom it can feed. When food is provided, it is easy to find the necessary clothing and lodging.[12]

> The number of workers increases with the increasing quantity of food or with the growing improvement and cultivation of land.[13]

Smith concludes (emphasis added):

> The cheapness and plenty of *good land* encourage improvement, and enable the proprietor to pay those high wages. In those wages consists almost the whole price of land; and though they are high, considered as the wages of labor, they are low, considered as the price of what is so very valuable. What encourages the progress of population and improvement encourages that of *real wealth* and greatness.[14]

Smith's argument is complete. Hunger drives cultivation. If endowed with good land, cultivation generates excess income, demand for nonnecessities, and improvement. Using similar logic, economic geographers attribute low levels of development in some, especially equatorial countries, to soil infertility.

While these supply-side considerations certainly have impact (as witnessed during the dust bowl of the 1930s in the United States), equation 3.5 dictates that even if soil fertility were very high on the equator (or infertile in the temperate climes), steady-state comfort would ultimately drive the equilibrium (progress). This is the primary distinction between a physioeconomic perspective and one of pure economic geography. Latitude is not geographical, it is physiological.

In this way, the question of interest is whether countries with similar dispositions will have converging absolute steady states of consumption or "food wants." Here is where Smith, and certain modern-day economic geographers (e.g., noting the infertility of certain tropical soils), differ from equation 3.5 by assuming homogenous preferences. Smith, for example, felt that the demand for food is constant across individuals and "is limited in every man by the narrow capacity of the human stomach,"[15] and that "the rich man consumes no more food that his poor neighbor. In quality it may be very different, and to select and prepare it may require more labor and art; but in quantity it is very nearly the same."[16] Montesquieu, on the other hand, uses reasoning more in line with equation 3.5, as he focused more on demand across geographies with differing steady-state thermodynamics:

> In hot countries, relaxation of the fibers produces a great perspiration of liquids, but solids dissipate less. The fibers, which have only a very weak action and little spring, are scarcely used; little nutritious juice is needed to repair them; thus one eats little there.[17]

Though his physiological reasoning was speculative, Montesquieu foresaw that increases in temperature leads to increases in steady-state fluid consumption and decreases in caloric consumption. To Montesquieu, even if bananas were easy to pick from the trees in all parts of the world, Germans would end up picking and eating more per capita in the steady state than Caribbeans. His conjecture is born out by modern-day experimental research, field studies, and cross-sectional times series.

Combining equation 3.5 with Smith, one would therefore expect that within-country variation in the distribution of food intake will be far less than the distribution of income (see Fogel, p. 373). Cross-country variance in aggregate food consumption, however, will remain divergent by thermal environment. Within any country, consumption will be invariant to dynamic changes in income after homeostatic equilibrium is reached in the steady state. Likewise, improvements in the production of food (per capita) will not increase consumption per capita after this point.

Over the last 250 years, some countries may have achieved the homeostatic steady state. Before that point, consumption dynamics would have (over the steep part of the consumption function) coincided with income changes. Fogel (p. 372), noted that "in 1790, the average caloric intake for Britains was about 2,060 calories and 1,753 calories in France," or about 30 to 40 percent below current levels. Fogel (p. 371) also notes that "recent research indicates that, for many European nations before the middle of the nineteenth century, the national production of food was at such low levels that the poorer classes were bound to have been malnourished under any conceivable circumstance, and the high disease rates of the period were not merely a cause of malnutrition but undoubtedly, to a considerable degree, a consequence of exceedingly poor diets." In the United States, "American males born during the first quarter of the nineteenth century were not only stunted by today's standards, but their BMI's [body mass index] at adult ages were about 15-percent lower than current U.S. levels." Fogel (p. 378)

Relying on the first law of thermodynamics, Fogel (p. 386) notes that the improvements in health and the increase in caloric consumption allowed greater energy to be spent on work and that "the intensity of work per hour has increased because of the number of calories available to work increased." Within Britain, he attributes from 20 to 50 percent of the growth rate to the increased energy supplied in caloric food energy, and draws a parallel between human physiology and thermodynamics. In contrast, the previous discussion would indicate that the higher caloric intakes were driven by exogenous motivations to increase comfort in line with equation 3.5. In essence, if warm and cold countries alike had the same caloric intake 200 years ago, the colder countries were less developed than the warmer countries. The former grew faster, as neoclassical growth models would predict, as these were farther from the steady state.

Clothing

As discussed in chapter 4, the right-hand side of the energy balance equation can relate to the consumption of clothing. As for food intake, the compensatory nature of the heat exchange equation makes it difficult to isolate thermal effects on clothing consumption. Overall, however, the statement on food by the FAO, above, can be rewritten as follows:

> That human beings [wear less clothes] in a hot climate than they do in a cold climate is generally recognized, but it is extremely difficult to express the relationship between climate and [clothing] needs quantitatively.

Some difficulties arise due to the heat exchange equation but also due to the dual purpose of clothing as being socially decorative (e.g., for self esteem, and courtship) and as protective insulation from the environment (see Cena and Clark 1979 for an early review, and Clark and Edholm, 1985, chapter 1, who discuss the effects of thermal conditions on clothing preferences). It turns out that thermal variations will tend to swamp social utilities derived from clothing as a baseline effect. In other words, all regions require clothes for social and decorative reasons, the shear quantity of material, irrespective of the design or branding involved, will systematically vary.

Physiologically, clothing was invented by humans to provide an insulation against excessive heat loss. The effectiveness of clothing as a thermal insulator is proportional to the thickness of the dead air enclosed (Burton and Edholm 1955). Windbreakers, for example, are designed to reduce heat loss via convection, by trapping warm still air close to the body. Clark and Edholm (1985, p. 200) describe fur coats as "consisting of very expensive air trapped between hair." The low conductivity of air requires that trapped air consist of relatively small cells (e.g., 0.5 cm^3) that remain immobile. Where multiple layers are used, air diffuses from one layer to the next in a "bellows" action.

The optimal clothing to achieve thermal comfort thus derives directly from the environment, whether indoor or outdoor. In hot environments, optimal clothing depends on the level of humidity. In outdoor hot desert environments, the clothing observed in North Africa and the Middle East consists of rather bulky, though voluminous, textiles that simultaneously protect the body from sand particles in the air and reflect solar radiation, but also act as billows to allow heat to be expelled in the resulting air stream. Bedouin Arabs also use the clothing as a thermal insulator during the colder evenings, when it is warn closer to the body. In tropic environs with high humidity, clothing impedes evaporative energy transfer, but can act to reflect solar radiation. Optimally, clothing, if worn at all in the tropics, should be worn loose and be made of lighter materials.

Clothing: Field Research

By far the most research in this area was conducted during and after WWII by various military forces, including the Institute for Aviation Medicine in England, and the Quartermaster Research Laboratories and the U.S. Army Research Institute of Environmental Medicine in the United States. These institutions have made painstaking efforts to quantify the physiological aspects of clothing and housing in an attempt to maintain troops and civilian personnel at optimal physical comfort, following acclimatization. Using rather precise measurements, researchers now understand the various insulative values for most garments and can predict, for both internal and external usage, homeostatic preferences for each type.

The insulative properties of clothing is measured in *clo*. One clo is typically defined as the insulation value of clothing that will allow convective and radiant heat transfer of 6.54 watts/°C for each degree of temperature difference between the skin and its surroundings (Goldman 1977, p. 169). Table 6.2 lists clo ratings for various clothing items. The minimal quantity of clothing required to meet social norms varies by thermal condition. As the ambient temperature declines, a tropical environment closer to the skin is recreated by adding clo. In cool situations, about .5 clo is typically required for social norms (i.e., covering most parts of the skin with reasonable insulation).

The thermally optimal attire in many tropical regions is to wear no clothing to encourage maximal evaporation at minimal discomfort. Social norms and skin protection often dictate a minimal level of clothing in certain tropical countries. In these places, the thermally optimal clothing is extremely light and "airy" to encourage evaporation. Table 6.3, based on military attire, considered "ensembles" that are recommended requirements for people working outdoors. As one approaches colder areas, the clothing requirement to achieve comfort exponentially changes similarly to metabolism for undressed persons in a climate chamber. Between 20°C and 30°C, little change in clothing are required as autonomic process can maintain relative comfort. Below 20°C, higher quantities

Table 6.2
Intrinsic insulation clo for civilian garments and footwear

Men's clothing	Clo	Women's clothing	Clo
Underpants	0.05	Bras and panties	0.05
Undershirt, sleeveless	0.06	Slip, half	0.13
Undershirt, "T"	0.09	Slip, full	0.19
Trousers, light	0.26	Slacks, light	0.26
Trousers, heavy	0.32	Slacks, heavy	0.44
Light shirt, short sleeve	0.14	Blouse, light	0.20
Light shirt, long sleeve	0.22	Blouse, heavy	0.29
Heavy shirt, short sleeve	0.25	Shirt, light	0.10
Heavy shirt, long sleeve	0.29	Shirt, heavy	0.22
Sweater, light	0.20	Sweater, light	0.17
Sweater, heavy	0.37	Sweater, heavy	0.37
Vest, light	0.15	Dress, light	0.20
Vest, heavy	0.29	Dress, heavy	0.63
Jacket, light	0.22	Jacket, light	0.17
Jacket, heavy	0.49	Jacket, heavy	0.37
Socks, ankle	0.04	Stockings, short	0.01
Socks, knee high	0.10	Panty hose	0.01
Shoes, sandals	0.02	Shoes, sandals	0.02
Shoes, oxfords	0.04	Shoes, pumps	0.04
Shoes, boots	0.08	Shoes, boots	0.08

Source: Adapted from Goldman 1977, p. 170.

Table 6.3

Military clothing from equatorial to polar conditions (net clo)

Military clothing	Clo-value	Climate
Ensembles (at still air layer approx. 0.7 clo)		
Coveralls, cotton with undershirt and shorts	0.6	Equatorial
Shirt and trousers, cotton, with undershirt and shorts	0.6	
Shirt and trousers, light wool with lightweight long underwear	1.0	
Shirt and trousers, heavy wool with medium weight long underwear	2.5	
Shirt and trousers, heavy wool, heavy long underwear, lined parka and hood	3.6	Polar
Handwear (at still air layer approx. 0.3 clo)		
Glove, light nylon, anticontact	0.05	Equatorial
Glove, leather, unlined	0.20	
Glove, wool	0.30	
Glove, leather and wool insert	0.45	
Mitten, wool	0.50	
Mitten shell light leather, light wool insert	0.90	
Mitten shell heavy leather, heavy wool insert	1.40	
Mitten shell heavy leather, heavy wool insert, with liner	1.90	Polar

Table 6.3 (continued)

Military clothing	Clo-value	Climate
Footwear (at still air layer approx. 0.5 clo)		
Sneakers, 1 pair of wool sox	0.2	Equatorial
Leather, low quarter wool sox	0.4	
Leather, 6" upper, wool sox	0.4	
Shoepack, leather upper, rubber bottom, wool sox	0.6	
Cold-wet insulated boot, wool sox	1.3	
Cold-dry insulated boot, wool sox	1.5	
Mukluk, felt duffle sox and wool sox	1.7	
Mukluk, quilted doubled duffle sox and wool sox	2.0	Polar

Source: Adapted from Goldman (1977, p. 172).

of clothing are required. People living in Canada, for example, who have any outside activity must wear up to ten times the clothing (in energy equivalents) to people residing on the equator. Again, this relationship exists irrespective of the social or variety-seeking behaviors of consumers. A person acclimatized to the tropics who has maximal clothing variety will consume less clothing than a similar person with similar variety preferences acclimatized to a temperate climate. This is all the more true when comparing regions that experience both tropical summers and severe winters. As long as people in these regions (e.g., the eastern United States) wish to venture out of doors, they will purchase and then consume, at C^*, both winter and summer clothing, whereas the person residing at the equator will generally only consume summer or warm weather clothing.

Clothing-Housing Interactions

As societies develop, there is a direct interaction between housing and optimal clothing for indoor usage (as suggested by equation 3.5). Housing also acts as an insulator and protective thermal barrier (or inhibitor). For this reason, the two are difficult to separate completely, and much research has been conducted to consider the optimal balance for humans.

The U.S. Army Research Institute of Environmental Medicine considered the interaction of external environment and internal heating and clothing requirements for the body to achieve thermal comfort for both civilian and military situations. Space limitations prevent a full summary of this research. The most important conclusion is that clothing and internal heating vary either by climate or by season in line with equation 3.5 for humans acclimatized to a given region. Office workers in New York City, for example, wear at their places of work approximately 0.6 clo in winter and 0.45 clo in summer (Gagge et al. 1976), and average preferred thermostat settings there in the summer are set from 23.3 to 26.7°C, versus approximately 20.5°C in winter.

According to Goldman (p. 172):

> Even wearing a total of 2.0 clo (i.e., 1.3 clo
> intrinsic) in winter, temperatures will have to be
> kept between 18 and 20°CET for comfort unless
> such drastic measures as wearing gloves, heavy
> footwear, and hats indoors are adopted and,
> even then, thermostats can probably not be set
> much below 15°C.

The type of interaction observed largely varies by the form
of optimal housing, to which the chapter now turns.

Housing

In the human time scale, housing is a relatively recent
phenomenon and was first "invented" to avoid climatic
conditions and to protect people from animal predators or
other humans. From ancient times to present, the forms of
housing have always varied by climate. The introduction of
internal air conditioning and heating has not changed this
pattern, but only allowed, for certain climates, better
adaptation or comfort. It is important to understand that
humans acclimatize to a given climate based on a limited
number of hours exposed to the external environment. In
this way, people in Sweden will still tend to consume more
calories of food than residents of the equator, even though
the former have built habitats that replicate equatorial
climates (unless, of course, they live entirely in doors, all
year long from birth). Similarly, people at the equator can

have a utility for cool air conditioning, however, they will set the thermostat to a higher temperature than a resident of New York City, who has been exposed to seven months of cool weather.

Physiology, then, indicates that people residing in areas that have extremely hot and humid summers, and extremely cold winters, will end up being driven (via the hypothalamus) to adapt the most. They undergo the largest thermal stress in the absence of artificial environments. In modern times, this has meant simultaneously installing indoor heating and air conditioning, thus expending the greatest amounts of artificial energy to maintain thermal comfort. These areas of the world include, for example, the Midwest and mid-Atlantic region of the United States. Other high latitude areas of the world have found it unnecessary to install internal air conditioning (e.g., northern Europe). Similarly, most of the world's inhabitants have not found it desirable to create housing with artificial internal heat. In other words, Singaporean income can converge to that of Finland, but the Finns will expend less of their basket on air conditioning and the Singaporeans will spend less on internal heating. Likewise, even in Finnish buildings with air conditioning, the Finns will set the thermostat to a cooler temperature than the Singaporeans who are acclimatized to the topics. The basket of goods consumed will never converge across countries even though incomes might.

Housing: Design Consumption

For a complete discussion on the effects of climate on optimal building and housing design, see Clark and Edholm (1985, chapter 11). Broadly speaking, housing and building requirements have been studied mostly for public buildings (e.g., elementary schools), military installations, and hospitals where optimal conditions are often seen as a critical element of design.

In colder environments, buildings are fundamentally designed to keep residents warm. In hotter climates, they are not designed to retain heat, and if appropriately conceived, can avoid large amounts of energy for cooling. In some climates where thermal comfort is closest to ambient temperatures, housing is designed to protect the residents from harsh weather and other environmental stresses, as opposed to preserving thermal comfort. To some extent, internal decoration is also related to thermoregulatory effects (e.g., bedding type, chair design, etc.), though this element has not received as much attention in the literature, except in cases of military or hospital environments, especially as this relates to neonatal care where temperature variations can be a critical element to survivability (Clark and Edholm, chapter 11).

Corresponding to the same result as that found for food and clothing, research has found that the statement by the FAO is applicable to housing:

> That human beings [consume less housing] in a
> hot climate than they do in a cold climate is
> generally recognized, but it is extremely
> difficult to express the relationship between
> climate and [housing] needs quantitatively.

Although architecture has long emphasized the role of
thermal conditions and climate on housing design,
physiologists have provided research more in line with
equation 3.5.

In optimal surface areas (walls), for example, the comfort
range depends on the types of clothing worn, the room's
surface radiation, and the individual's metabolism. Olesen
et al. (1972) recommends the following equation, to define
the limits of acceptable temperature differences between a
vertical surface and the average radiant temperature:

$$-2.4 - 1.8I_{cl} < \Delta t_w F_{p\text{-}w} < 3.9 + 1.8I_{cl} \qquad (6.1)$$

where Icl is the clo-value of clothing, $F_{p\text{-}w}$ is the angle factor
between a sedentary person and the vertical radiant area,
and Δt_w is the temperature difference (Kelvin) between the
radiant source and the mean radiant temperature in
relation to the individual. In essence, people can affect their
comfort levels by wearing more clothing to compensate for
a colder room surface.

Similarly, if one isolates the effects of footwear, one needs
to consider the duration over which the person prefers to

walk in bare feet and the optimal flooring. Again, there are
limits for people wearing footwear (Fanger, p. 149):

> If one accepts up to 8 percent uncomfortable, the
> floor temperature should be within the interval
> $22-30°C$ for sedentary and $20-28°C$ for
> standing or walking persons. At floor
> temperatures below $20-28°C$ the percentage of
> people experiencing cold feet generally
> increases rapidly. Although heavier clothing can
> provide thermal neutrality at a lower ambient
> temperature, there is a risk of cold discomfort at
> the feet, if they are not protected
> correspondingly by well-insulated footwear. If
> normal light footwear is worn, higher ambient
> temperatures will be required to counteract the
> coldness of feet.

At cold temperatures, consumption is required to achieve
comfort for all parts of the body where skin is exposed or
may transfer heat directly via conduction or convection
(e.g., head, hands, and feet).

Table 6.4, for example, considers the optimal
flooring/temperature combination for people walking bare
foot for 1 minute or 10 minutes. If one wishes to remain
comfortable and have the pleasure of walking barefoot at
low temperatures, a preferred flooring is pinewood. As
temperature increases, following the principles of
conduction in chapter 3, people will physiologically prefer

Table 6.4

Optimal flooring and temperature (°C)

Flooring	Occupancy 1 minute	Occupancy 10 minutes	Optimal recommended
Pinewood	25	25	22.5—28
Oakwood	26	26	24.5—28
PVS-sheet with felt underlay on concrete	28	27	24.5—28
Hard linoleum on wood	28	26	24—28
5mm tessellated floor on gas concrete	29	27	26—28.5
Concrete floor	28.5	27	26—28.5
Marble	30	29	28—29.5

Source: Adapted from Fanger (1977, p. 145).

a concrete floor or marble. Given the ground's conductive properties, clay or dirt floors frequently observed in low-income countries have long been an optimal architectural adaptation to thermal conditions. Similarly, thatched roofs and walls made of palm encourage evaporative and convective heat loss.

Housing: Aggregation

The above discussion only applies to the part of housing that is consumption (as opposed to savings). To attain the same level of comfort from housing consumption, one observes dramatic variations in housing styles across the world's physical environments. To modern architects, the idea that the utility for any specific aspect of a house's architecture is homogenous across all countries of the world would nicely be seen as heresy. If housing is broken down to its components, for a given square footage, it may contain a foundation, walls, electrical/telecommunications wiring and plumbing, heating and air conditioning systems, flooring, doors and windows, various fixtures, the ceiling, roof, insulation, crawl spaces, internal and external wall coverings, and landscaping. With the exception of certain fixtures and wiring, virtually all of the rest of what makes a house or apartment optimal for habitation varies across countries or more specifically climates.

There is nothing that would deterministically prevent, for example, Swedes from installing air-cooling systems for their homes, nor Singaporeans from installing heating. The utilities in doing so are, nevertheless, different across the two countries. The same logic holds for the optimal types of windows used, the distance from the ground foundation to the flooring and its type, the types of flooring, the thickness and materials used to make external and internal walls, the ability for air to flow from the natural environment through the walls and/or across the ceilings, and even the color of paint have all received substantial attention in architecture. The fundamental drivers here are the cost or benefit of materials and environmental physiology (see, for example, Clark and Edholm 1985, chapter 11).

In summary, the literature finds that the farther one's environment deviates from the human genetically evolved tropical set point, the greater is consumption required to achieve thermal homeostasis. The relation shown in figure 6.1 indicates, aggregating across all items, that homeostatic consumption in line with equation 3.5 will increase exponentially as the ambient temperature falls much below 20°C to 25°C.

Psychological Consumption

In *The Spirit of the Laws,* Montesquieu speculated that latitude would not only affect consumption of basic or thermal necessities but also a variety of other consumption behaviors, morals, crime rates, and suicide rates. The following passages illustrate his thoughts on certain forms of consumption, again, based on quasi-scientific observation and reasoning:

> In cold countries, one will have little sensitivity to pleasures; one will have more of it in temperate climates; in hot countries, sensitivity will be extreme. As one distinguishes climates by degrees of latitude, one can also distinguish them by degrees of sensitivity, so to speak. I have seen operas in England and Italy; they are the same plays with the same actors: but the same music produces such different effects in the people of the two nations that it seems inconceivable, the one so calm and the other so transported.[18]

> In northern climates, the physical aspect of love has scarcely enough strength to make itself felt; in temperate climates, love, accompanied by a thousand accessories, is made pleasant by things that at first seem to be love but are still not love; in hotter climates, one makes love for itself; it is the sole cause of happiness; it is life.[19]

> We see in the histories that the Romans did not inflict death on themselves without cause, but the English resolve to kill themselves when one can imagine no reason for their decisions; they kill themselves in the very midst of happiness. ... It is clear that the civil laws of some countries have had reasons to stigmatize the murder of oneself, but in England one can no more punish it than one can punish the effects of madness.[20]

Without question, the literature has revealed that chemical homeostasis equally applies to psychological balance (Powles 1992). It is equally true that suicide rates vary with latitude (i.e., high income countries have higher age-weighted rates of suicide); the simple correlation reported across studies varies (from 0.5 to 0.7), but is highly significant as long as equatorial countries are included in the sample; see Parker (1995) for a review. It is generally accepted now that this regularity, and seasonal affective disorder discussed in chapter 4, are both related to the lack of natural sunlight, or the low levels of luminosity experienced in the higher latitudes. Various neurochemical imbalances (e.g., serotonin, dopamine, etc.) are now thought to reach their maxima toward the end of the winter-spring seasons in the Northern Hemisphere and in the summer-fall in the Southern Hemisphere.

With the caveat that this is an emerging area of research, it can be conjectured that humans facing these imbalances will be more likely to seek remedy than those not so affected. The probability that this will occur, for any given individual, varies by latitude. Remedies include artificial light and stimulation. While it is true that various forms of entertainment consumption (e.g., television, personal computers, personal stereo) are highly seasonal and, across countries, are often better explained by latitude than by income, at this stage it is not clear that these forms of consumption are not simply driven by the fact that residents in these areas remain in doors (i.e., based on the thermal effect).[21]

It is nevertheless interesting to note that in a typical summer, some 67 percent of German's leave their country on vacation to warmer climates. The Mediterranean island of Majorca alone has some 2.2 million seasonal German residents every year.[22] Similarly, in a study reported by Gould and White (1974), British residents were simply asked: "Where would you like to be?" The gradient map, representing the frequency of respondents, showed a strong preference for living on the southern shore of the United Kingdom. In essence, whether due to psychological or purely thermal reasons, even short-run migration behavior shows spatial correlation: people seek warmer climes on vacation if they come from the higher latitudes.

As entertainment and vacation expenses form a small part of income across most developed countries, the motivations for such consumption will not likely drive the wide swings in income observed in present-day data.

Ethnic Differences

Both Montesquieu and Smith note that Europeans and more so their children tend to take on the consumption habits of the local climate. On alcohol consumption, for example, Smith's observations parallel those of Montesquieu (cited in chapter 1):

> The inhabitants of the wine countries are in general the soberest people in Europe; witness the Spaniards, the Italians, and the inhabitants of the southern provinces of France. People are seldom guilty of excess in what is their daily fare. On the contrary, …, drunkenness is a common vice, as among the northern nations.[23]

Smith further notes:

> When a French regiment comes from some of the northern provinces of France, where wine is somewhat dear, to be quartered in the southern, where it is very cheap, the soldiers, I have

> frequently heard it observed, are at first
> debauched by the cheapness and novelty of the
> good wine; but after a few months' residence the
> greater part of them become as sober as the rest
> of the inhabitants.[24]

Such observations, that individuals acclimatize to local
conditions, are important in understanding that the effects
of equation 3.5 are universal, independent of individual
disposition, culture, race, or ethnic origin.

Since the works of Montesquieu and Smith, a variety of
studies provide similar insights into the effects of genetic
variations on the principles above. These have involved
measuring the consumption habits of people migrating
from one region to another and comparing behaviors with
those of long-term residents (e.g., comparing members of
polar expeditions to residents of the arctic regions; see Folk
et al. 1998). Others consider people of different races living
in similar climatic conditions (see Clark and Edholm 1985,
chapter 7). Difficulties in controlling for culture, income
levels, and other nonclimatic factors make these hard to
interpret. One such study, however, considered Yemenite
and Kurdish Jews who lived in adjacent villages leading
similar lifestyles and in similar houses. Despite the two
having substantial ethnic and anthropometric differences,
the two groups showed very similar acclimatization and
food intakes (Fox et al. 1973). Based on a survey of studies,
Clark and Edholm (1985, p. 152−153) conclude that while
some genetic factors might contribute to some variances in

acclimatization, they are dominated by environmental factors. Similar findings are reported in Hanna et al. (1989) and Folk (1974, p. 136−215).

Summary

Experimental, field, and cross-sectional time series support the notion that homeostatic utility functions exist and imply a consumption plateau. That plateau exists in the aggregate across food, clothing, and forms of housing, and perhaps certain other goods generating purely psychological benefits (e.g., entertainment, psychotherapy, and related mental health care). If the zone of comfort varies from one spatial or thermal location to another, then one can expect marginal utilities to equate at different levels of consumption.

As long as the earth remains a sphere receiving solar energy, physics indicates that long-run utility and consumption patterns for homeostatic goods, as aggregate complements, will never converge across all countries. Physiological mechanisms, traceable to the workings of the hypothalamus, have been shown to react in line with the laws of thermodynamics at the individual and social levels. This has been demonstrated for both humans and other homeotherms by scientific experimentation (e.g., using climate chambers), field research (e.g., military studies), and cross-country statistics (e.g., food intake). No study, as yet, contradicts this finding. No controlled study ever will.

If you doubt that these effects are substantial, simply turn the thermostat in your home to the winter settings during the summer and vice versa. Furthermore, wear your winter clothing during the summer and vice versa; similarly for diet. For many, the laws of physics and hypothalmic reactions will result in physiological misery or possibly death for those willing to undertake such an experiment. As dictated by equation 3.5, however, the result of this experiment varies depending on how geographically close you live to the equator or to a climate having constant ambient temperatures approaching our genetically evolved tropical set point of approximately 25°C to 30°C.

As homeostatic goods include food, clothing and housing, or the three greatest wants of humans, these physioeconomic effects should not be discounted as noise. These effects, in fact, are the baseline around which political economy, especially bad policies, can generate substantial deviations to the detriment or benefit of populations. The equatorial paradox is not a random outcome resulting from corruption that might be coincidentally correlated with temperature. The paradox will persist well after tropical diseases are eradicated, tropical soils are made fertile, and economic, business and political institutions are optimized for general welfare. It will persist well after corruption, despotism, illiteracy, and malnutrition are eliminated altogether across all countries and life expectancies reach their biological limits everywhere. This would be true even if incomes were to somehow converge in the long run (i.e., the basket of goods consumed will remain divergent). Combined with supply-side effects (e.g., the existence of some forms of agriculture bounded by climatic zones), trade patterns, relative prices, the existence of product markets, and many behaviors incorrectly attributed to race or culture will always be endogenous to these thermodynamic effects.

The most important implication of this reality is that for the world to converge in economic performance, in terms of meeting basic human needs or providing comfortable standards of living, there will be a distribution of homeostatic consumption patterns across countries. The goal of development agencies, in this regard, is to help countries achieve consumption levels within a world-wide distribution and not to have all countries reach a unique level of consumption or income deemed "developed." In a world where the basket of homeostatic goods consumed will never converge, neither revealed preferences nor consumption can not be indicators of well being. Failing to consider this may lead to erroneous standards by which countries with certain consumption patterns are casually labeled "backward" or "advanced."

Likewise, criticisms of development agencies which have failed to equalize aggregate measures of consumption or income across countries are misplaced. Ranking the relative performance of countries based on their absolute levels of consumption or income is fundamentally flawed. In the long run, lesser developed countries cannot be identified by finding that these have lower levels of consumption vis-à-vis other countries. Likewise, highly developed countries may be incorrectly identified as such by virtue of these having high levels of consumption. If the aforementioned conclusions are true, then how can one measure the economic progress of a country or the effect of political economy using traditional metrics that ignore these systematic variances? To answer this, a few suggestions are made in the next chapter.

Notes

1. Smith (p. 128).

2. These consumption items were previously labeled *physiological hygiene* goods in the 1940s.

3. The early textbook of Winslow and Herrington (1949) directly considered how the consumption of goods such as clothing, housing, food, and health care will necessarily be affected by the physiology of equation 3.5 in chapter 3. The authors preface their thoughts with the conclusion that "climate and season remain among the most important factors in human health and welfare. (p. ix)

4. The authors average the results from Yoshimura (1969) and Wyndham (1964). Figures are indexed on a 0 to 100 percent scale using a monotonic transformation of the absolute range of metabolism recorded.

5. See Parker (1995).

6. Jane E. Brody, "Jack Sprat Could Eat No Fat, So He Gained Weight," International Herald Tribune, May 26, 1999, p. 1, 10.

7. Smith (p. 128).

8. Ibid. (p. 128).

9. Ibid. (p. 131).

10. Ibid. (p. 140).

11. Ibid. (p. 139).

12. Ibid. (p. 130).

13. Ibid. (p. 131).

14. Ibid. (p. 437).

15. Ibid. (p. 131).

16. Ibid. (p. 131).

17. Montesquieu (p. 239).

18. Ibid. (p. 233).

19. Ibid. (p. 234).

20. Ibid. (pp. 241 – 242).

21. Based on data reported in *European Marketing Data and Statistics*, and *International Marketing Data and Statistics* Euromonitor, various issues. For example, personal stereo is correlated .84, and personal computers is .60 (*p-values*<.0001) with absolute latitude.

22. Rick Atkinson, "Endless Run for the Sun Keeps German

Tourists on the Go," *International Herald Tribune*, July 29, 1999, p. 8.

23. Smith (p. 376).

24. Ibid. (p. 376).

7   Measuring Performance

The differing needs of differing climates have formed differing ways of living.

—Montesquieu[1]

Economics has long been at a disadvantage vis-à-vis the natural sciences. First, perfectly controlled country-level experiments with replication are essentially impossible. Relying on the natural experiment observed in cross-country economic statistics requires that one minimally control for sample heterogeneity. Identifying exogenous factors generating this heterogeneity is not obvious. Second, if one concedes that consumer utility (satisfaction, or comfort) is an essential part of economic development, economics finds itself at a point in history similar to thermodynamics in mid-seventeenth century: it does not have a causal model of heat, nor a good thermometer. Microeconomics might do without either; in economic growth, they may be essential.

The goal of this chapter is to *suggest* ideas for relative performance indicators (RPI), in the absence of direct measures of cardinal utility, as well as recommend future avenues for empirical research. The intent is to isolate the effects of political economy, while controlling for differences in utility or geographic disposition. In doing so, one may determine the extent to which long-run growth is due to certain economic policies, versus inherent human motivations driven by the exogenous forces of nature. Ideally, new measures could easily be integrated into existing models of growth that assume their performance measures to be utility constant.

Problems with Unique Standards

The fact that many consumption patterns or, in Montesquieu's parlance, "ways of living" will predictably vary in line with the equatorial paradox, based on the physics of heat transfer, is a fundamental empirical generalization with direct policy implications. In *The Limits to Growth*, the Club of Rome made dire predictions on the future state of human nutrition. Rather innocuous assumptions were critical to their conclusions (Meadows et al. 1974, p. 57): "Lines indicating calories and proteins required are those estimated for North Americans."

In assuming an absolute global standard, the authors claimed that residents the world over have identical steady-state levels of consumption and that the North American level represented "developed." In particular, they assumed that development implied achieving the same body mass as North Americans rather than focusing on voluntary (unconstrained) intake or on the nutritional requirements for full mental and/or physical functions and comfort. The estimated shortfall of calories and protein from the steady state in the warmer regions of the world was massive. While malnutrition and food shortages occur in many low-income countries, by assuming a unique global standard, the urgency for long-run food transfer to the warmer areas of the planet (mostly from subsidized farms in western Europe and North America) overshadowed the possibility that food aid might destroy local farming economies supplying adequate caloric needs at a lower steady state. The following news item is typical of many in this regard:

> Citing a 'dangerous moment' for hard pressed American farmers, President Bill Clinton announced that the government would buy wheat worth $250 million to boost farmers' prices. ... The wheat will be donated as humanitarian relief in [Africa] and elsewhere.[2]

This policy was designed to raise the U.S. price per bushel by 13 cents, not to meet nutritional requirements of the peoples of Africa nor stabilize farm-gate prices for farmers there. Food aid and expertise surely should be granted with the primary goal of meeting both short- and long-term homeostatic needs (reduce deprivation, stunting and wasting) and not inflating the prices of sellers in high-income countries. While malnutrition and food shortfalls mostly are apparent in low-income countries, only by knowing homeostatic standards will policymakers realize that lower consumption levels in some countries do not automatically imply a need or justify subsidized external transfers.

Since absolute values of revealed consumption are ambiguous, setting standards, whether global or local, is hazardous. Low or high levels of consumption may signal either deprivation, comfort, or super satiation, depending on where consumption falls on the homeostatic utility function. One needs to have measures (broken down by age and gender) of the minimal expenditures required for a comfortable life. Ideally, one would like to know the consumption level where marginal utilities roughly equate for the homeostatic aspects of housing, food, clothing, and energy, across all countries of the world and within all regions of each country. These levels should allow for the fact that body mass will typically increase as populations are better nourished. For any given body mass, this mass may not lead to equal levels of consumption.

Once a basic relationship has been established between spatial location and long-run consumption steady states, many years of work will be required to generate commonly accepted and comparable standards that might reflect equivalence in comfort for any specific good (e.g., clothing items, housing items, food items, etc.). The following ideas, therefore, are hardly definitive and substantial resources should be devoted to more careful study.

Idea 1: Exploiting Spatial Correlation

Econometric Problems

Empirical studies require that the observations studied be independent from each other and the statistics calculated from these observations be independent. Violations in these assumptions can be observed in the values of the observations themselves, or in the residuals of regression models. As discussed in chapter 2, spatial autocorrelation arises in cross-country economic research because the units of observations are scattered in geographic space and are not totally independent from one another. This form of correlation has its parallels in times-series analysis and in particular serial autocorrelation. In both cases, failure to control or account for these correlations results in inefficient parameter estimates, biased estimates of significance, and bad inferences (Anselin 1988). If a spatial explanatory variable is correlated with both income and factors felt to affect income, its omission leads not only to inefficient estimators but biased estimates as well for the included variables (as with other specification errors or omitted variables problems). Simply including latitude in a traditional growth equation, therefore, is not advisable. Rather, one might be better served by somehow filtering or adjusting the left-hand side of the equation, as done for purchasing power parities, or distortions in exchange rates.

Intuition

The observation that international economic observations are spatially correlated is well known but rarely considered explicitly. Intuitively, consider the possibility that the fifty states of the United States each became independent countries admitted to the United Nations in the year 2000. If one started with 188 observations before 1999, does one now have 238 independent observations in 2000? Clearly the theoretical degrees of freedom (independent observations) are far less than 238. Shared histories and educational standards, among other factors, affect economic measures across these new countries. How many *real* degrees of freedom current studies have today is, in the absence of correction, an open question.

The practical implication of spatial correlation lies in the possibility that inferences are manifestly incorrect or exaggerated. Consider, for example, a simple study that seeks to determine the historical effects of communism on growth. Using a dummy variable, noncommunist countries are coded as zero and communist countries as one. In theory, one would expect the estimated coefficient in a regression on income to yield a negative and statistically significant coefficient: communism lowers income per capita. In reality, however, the result is disappointing.[3] Similar disappointment is found when one considers the effects of socialist policies where private ownership is allowed. Indeed, such obvious policy variables would be natural for cross-country econometric models. How can a dummy variable for communism be marginally significant, or worse, yield the wrong sign when communism manifestly lowers incomes? The reason lies in the fact that there are far more poor capitalist countries (mostly in the tropics) than wealthy capitalist countries, and most communist countries experienced higher long-run growth rates since WWII compared to the low-income capitalist countries.

Sample Matching

Prior to the fall of the Berlin wall, income per capita in many, especially European, communist countries exceeded those of equatorial capitalist countries in Africa, Latin America, and Asia. Simply regressing communism against income (with or without other variables) is unacceptable. To obtain a plausible result, one can exploit the fact that observations must be spatially correlated in the steady state (i.e., homeostatic utilities will be similar from one thermally adjacent country to another). By using paired comparisons of proximate observations in physioeconomic space, the correct result can be obtained. In this case one would need to compare North to South Korea, East to West Germany, Togo to Benin, Jamaica to Cuba, and so on. In doing so, one has essentially "filtered" for steady-state spatial correlation generated by physioeconomic factors.

While many economic phenomena appear to follow Tobler's first law of geography that "everything is related to everything else, but near things are more related than distant things," the previous chapters suggest that it is thermal distance that matters, not proximity. In other words, one can compare the economy of the United States to that of Russia or New Zealand, even though the countries are distant in geographic space. Likewise, policies leading to growth successes in one area of the world may be uncovered that prove useful in other areas with similar steady states, even though these might be located on the other side of the planet. In this regard, thermal spatial correlation implies that expertise is likely to vary by latitude (i.e., expertise for success may not come from the higher latitudes for the lower latitudes). This has certainly proven to be the case for most things relating to architecture, clothing, nutrition, and agriculture.

Implementation

Lacking the equivalent of monozygotic twins across countries implies that sample matching in practice will never be perfect. It is, however, far better than assuming that all countries are identical in exogenous factors that might affect growth. With this caveat, one can start by clustering countries based on their physioeconomic dispositions. Within each cluster, asymmetric spatial correlations are effectively eliminated. Countries within each can then be ranked by various measures of performance, or standard econometric modeling can be applied. Some of the larger countries may need to be decomposed into smaller regions as if they were countries (e.g., for Brazil, the United States, Russia, India, and

China). Successful growth or welfare policies would more likely than not be revealed in those ranking high for particular measures of progress. For example, if each country is clustered by broad climatic types (as identified in Parker 1997d), one finds countries such as Togo being clustered with Costa Rica revealing the following comparison:

Variable	Togo	Costa Rica
Latitude (absolute degrees)	8	10
Land area (k sq km)	56.8	51.1
Population (m)	4.9	3.6
Life expectancy (years)	59	76
Infant mortality (per 1000)	79.8	13.1
Adult literacy (%)	52	95
GDP/capita (ppp)	$1,300	$5,500

Though Costa Rica has very low income compared to high income countries with similar population sizes (e.g., Denmark at $23,200), it represents a major growth success (controlling for thermal spatial correlation). In this light, countries such as Costa Rica, as opposed to the United States or other OECD economies, merit far more attention than their raw income statistics would indicate. In the case of Costa Rica, large investments in health and education, at the expense of a military, and tropic-based exports in agriculture and tourism ("exporting" its latitude) cannot be ignored as a basic model of development for countries in its cluster. The conjecture implied by this type of analysis is that if countries within a cluster can somehow transfer "best practice," the room for future growth is substantial.

The application of sample matching to the other major climatic zones, used by environmental physiologists mentioned in chapter 4, reveals similar successes-failures with the most obvious conclusion being that communism (and its lingering effects) was a disastrous economic model. The country ranked lowest within the temperate climate cluster is North Korea (at $900 income per capita), as seen in the following comparison:

Variable	North Korea	South Korea
Latitude (absolute degrees)	40	37
Land area (k sq km)	120	98
Population (m)	21.2	46.4
Life expectancy (years)	51	74
Infant mortality (per 1000)	87.8	7.8
Adult literacy (%)	99	98
GDP/capita (ppp)	$900	$13,700

For future growth prospects, this procedure has the useful artifact in revealing a present-day development frontier to which all countries in the cluster can aspire. Although the frontier might shift over time, due to changes in technology or the state of knowledge, countries with highest performance are closest to the prevailing frontier.

Dynamics

Applying diminishing returns to investments designed to achieve largely biological limits (e.g., infant mortality, life expectancy, and literacy), one knows that countries farthest from the frontier will grow faster over time than those closer to the frontier, as long as they transfer successful policies. For the temperate cluster, North Korea will have the fastest growth rate (improvements) in infant mortality and life expectancy, should the regime there adopt the political economy of the more successful members in its cluster. It will also be the next century's growth miracle for income per capita to the extent that income is dominated by homeostatic goods and services. North Korea's misery will sadly be its hypothalmic growth motivation leading to the liberalization of its economy, high savings, long work hours, investments, and entrepreneurship. North Korea will not grow, however, in adult literacy, as it is already at the frontier. Similar transformations are now transpiring in most of central and eastern Europe and China (especially above 30°N latitude). In the long-run, transition friction observed in places like Russia will be swamped by the more fundamental motivations affecting its residents.

Idea 2: Statistical Filtering

Although establishing cluster membership may prove problematic, the revelation of policy is a clear advantage of exploiting the asymmetric spatial correlations observed in cross-country economic statistics. A shortcoming of that approach is the limited insight that might be obtained "within" each cluster. An alternative approach involves filtering cross-country data for exogenous climatic variables, as one might deseasonalize time series data prior to measuring the impact of policy. In this way, all countries are considered simultaneously, and "success" stories are estimated across all physioeconomic dispositions.

Intuition

Cross-sectional filtering of economic data is not an obvious exercise, especially given the large number of factors that might affect current dispersions in income per capita. The least problematic method may be simply to let the data do the talking. Basically, one can regress purely exogenous and invariant factors against each development indicator and use the residuals as indicators of performance. The goal is not to find out which country is higher or lower on the given measure (the variable speaks for itself), but rather to discover how it is that some arrive at higher levels than others given unequal starting positions that drive and correlate with long-run steady states. Of course, homeostatic efforts are confounded with purely geographic supply-side effects (e.g., disease, or soil depletion found in certain areas of the tropics).

Figure 7.1 reveals why using variables beyond thermal indicators may be desirable. This figure plots gross domestic product (GDP) per capita across 171 countries from 1970 to 1995.[4] Five countries appear to have

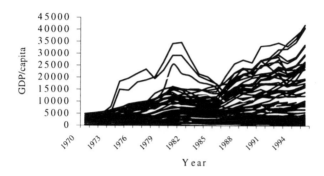

Figure 7.1
GDP/capita for 171 countries (current USD): 1970–1995

experienced "growth miracles" that might be considered models of development by others. If one were to limit the study to the period 1970 to 1980, one might have concluded that growth is substantially a function of a country's ability to form international resource-based cartels. The top five countries shown in 1980 are Qatar, United Arab Emirates (UAE), Brunei, and Saudi Arabia. As the figure indicates, this remarkable resource-based growth was ephemeral. By 1995, all of these countries saw their incomes shrink, the rents exploited from economic geography being reduced by competition. By 1995, all were surpassed by Italy and the wealthiest among these, the UAE, had roughly the GDP per capita of Ireland. Similar episodes in history have existed for other countries or city states due to their strategic locations or mineral wealth (e.g., Australia at the turn of the century, Venice or Mali in the fourteenth century). Natural resources, per se, while certainly providing short-run arbitrage opportunities, do not appear to be the basis for long-run economic growth. Nevertheless, at any moment in human history, natural resources have affected the form and cross-sectional variance of wealth and cannot be discarded out of hand.[5]

Implementation

Combined, exogenous factors (e.g., dummy variables for each religion, natural reserves for each rare mineral, etc.) that might affect growth can be greater than the number of observations under study. This is especially true if one limits the study to a region, such as Europe. This problem can be mitigated by exploiting the natural causal ordering across filters, using a type of step-down analysis (as opposed to step-wise regression) whereby each filter is applied in sequence of exogeneity. The explained variance across filters, then, reveals the incremental impact of each in explaining variances beyond exogenous factors previously considered.

Figure 7.2 describes one filtering procedure, among many one might consider, that proves useful in considering both thermal and nonthermal factors. It combines elements of physiology (for long-run effects) and economic geography (to control for endowment-based effects). This is not the only way one might choose to filter development indicators for exogenous factors. Figure 7.3, for example, is adapted from Diamond's (1997) model of how economic geography

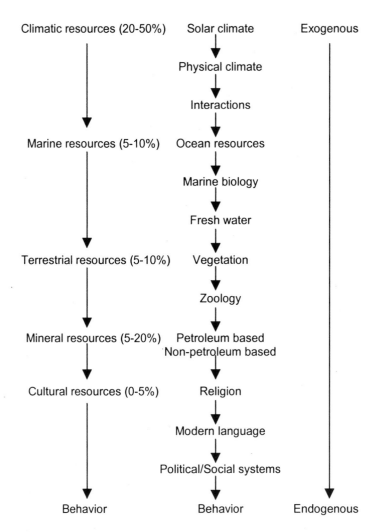

Figure 7.2
Exogenous filters by causal hierarchy (typical incremental explained variance across production and consumption measures in parentheses; adapted from Parker 1997d)

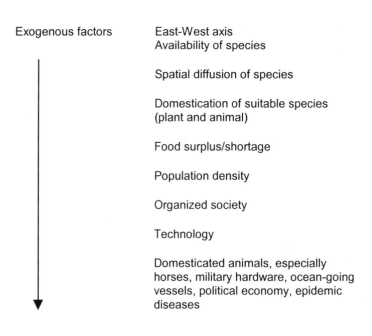

Exogenous factors   East-West axis
                           Availability of species

                           Spatial diffusion of species

                           Domestication of suitable species
                           (plant and animal)

                           Food surplus/shortage

                           Population density

                           Organized society

                           Technology

                           Domesticated animals, especially
                           horses, military hardware, ocean-going
                           vessels, political economy, epidemic
                           diseases

Endogenous factors

Figure 7.3
Model of economic geography (adapted from Diamond 1997)

affected development across countries. The key difference
between figures 7.2 and 7.3 is the strict ordering observed
in the former which places thermodynamic and
physiological steady states as the primal driver of
variances. In the presence of technology, global diffusion
and reduced transportation costs, geographic factor
endowments (such as oil or minerals) perturb growth to
the steady state, but do not alter the steady state that is
largely biological and exogenous to those endowments.

Table 7.1 shows the results of sequential filters on a variety of development items that are likely to reflect, at least in part, homeostatic consumption.[6] Filters cover six broad areas following a hierarchy of exogeneity, established by natural historians, whereby certain natural phenomenon are necessary conditions (and simultaneously historical precedents) to others lower in the hierarchy. Climate, for example, is a necessary condition for marine and animal-human life, which in turn is a necessary condition for culture. Solar climate is the most exogenous of factors in natural history. Physical climate follows (continental formation), resulting in land and ocean topology; again, without solar climate, physical climates would not exist. Climatic forces are then held to be responsible for variances in the world's natural marine biology, vegetation, and zoological resources, in that order. Here again, without marine biology, vegetation resources would be absent and so forth for zoological resources. Minerals are then considered exogenous to these as their observance and creation is predicated on plant and animal existence. Culture is the most endogenous; modern religions are generally held to be more exogenous than modern languages. Although it is clear that solar climate remains the absolute necessary condition, it is not clear that culture is a necessary condition to modern political economy that we will assume to be endogenous to religion and language.

A variety of variables can measure each of the above. In what follows, all of the relevant statistics are reported in Parker (1997d) for 234 countries and territories. For the

Table 7.1

Exogenous filters across development measures (incremental explained variances)

	Climate	Marine	Terrestrial	Mineral	Cultural
Food					
Beer	0.44	0	0	0	0
Calories	0.52	0	0	0	0
Cheese	0.42	0	0	0	0
Eggs	0.28	0	0	0	0
Pork	0.66	0	0.02	0	0
Potatoes	0.42	0	0	0	0
Rice	0.51	0	0	0	0
Wine	0.23	0	0.14	0	0
Non-food					
Inflation	0	0	0	0	0
Newsprint	0.44	0.04	0.01	0	0
Telephone/capita	0.51	0.02	0.02	0	0.01
Television/captia	0.43	0.05	0	0	0
Steel	0.55	0	0	0	0
Suicide	0.42	0.1	0	0	0
Production					
Wool production	0.87	0	0	0	0
Diamonds	0.17	0	0	0.62	0
Tin	0.24	0	0	0.48	0
Bauxite	0.38	0	0	0.42	0.05

Note: Data reported in Parker (1997d) and Euromonitor, International Data and Statistics CD 1998.

sake of illustration, solar climate was measured as a simple nonlinear transformation of absolute latitude (e.g., the exponential of latitude). Physical climate is measured by a country's elevation and total land area, which accounts for some land-mineral endowments. Interactions are measured via dummy variables for climatic classifications (which capture variances in meteorology). Marine resources are measured using fresh water supply, coastline length, and the existence of a natural deep-water harbor. Land, vegetation, and zoological resources were captured using biome classifications and tectonic dummies. Mineral resources are measured by natural oil reserves and the number of rare minerals present. Culture measures include percentages for the five largest world religions, number of ethnic groups present, and the use of major colonial languages. To evaluate the robustness of the empirics, various alternative measures, also reported in Parker (1997d) were used for each level of the hierarchy. Although the results are fairly insensitive to various changes in definitions (e.g., whether using a square of latitude, its exponential, or temperature, etc.), there is certainly room for improvement over the ones illustrated here.

As shown in table 7.1, climate explains a substantial portion of variance across countries for many items (the equatorial paradox). Across all of the measures, culture (e.g., religious or linguistic) explains little of the variance after the data have been previously filtered for more fundamental drivers (confirming Montesquieu's conjecture that religion has little net effect and is both endogenous to and confounded with climate).

Likewise, many of the measures are only marginally affected by factor endowments often noted by economic geographers (e.g., mineral resources explain only 3 percent of income variances). This arises because substantial variations are seen in behavior across countries with similar levels of endowment, and this variance (explained by more exogenous factors) swamps the variances created by the endowments themselves. Of those countries rich in natural oil reserves, for example, the high-income countries include Norway, Canada, and the United States with incomes per capita exceeding $15,000, while the poorest countries include Nigeria, India, Yemen, and Senegal, all with incomes below $2,000. The correlation between oil production per capita and income for non-OPEC countries is not statistically significant (.04; not significant) whereas for countries within OPEC, the correlation is high and statistically significant (.92, *p-value*<.01). The difference between these two groups is one of diversity. OPEC members are heavily endowed with oil (the higher the production per capita, the higher the income per capita), whereas non-OPEC member economies are more diversified. While one cannot ignore this source of wealth, it only perturbs the baseline effect of latitude. Furthermore, oil-based wealth does not necessarily affect homeostatic consumption. This is readily seen by the fact that oil wealth does not show up as affecting caloric intake, for example, after climate has been filtered. Mineral wealth, however, does affect production in minerals, as might be expected.

Relative Performance

The primary interest here is not to consider the importance of the exogenous factors but rather the potential insights from the final residuals after the development measures have been fully filtered. This residual is an RPI as it controls for exogenous factors that would parallel systematic differences in steady states of homeostatic utility. Table 7.2, for a sample of countries, shows an RPI across countries as indicated by the filtered GDP per capita in 1992. Countries with high residuals, or RPIs, are high performers (i.e., have higher outputs, given their exogenous situations), compared to those with low RPIs.

As table 7.2 indicates, relative performance is not related to absolute income per capita; the filtered residual is uncorrelated to income per capita (p-$value$>.25). Highest performers have residuals that are two or more deviations from the mean, and so forth for the other categories. Again, despite the United States having over 400 percent more income per capita, one finds that it has lower relative performance than Costa Rica. Similarly, Burkina Faso is an above average performer, given its starting position, compared to the United States. In other words, Burkina Faso has been better at generating more income given its steady-state endowments than the United States has with its endowments. This is a sobering conclusion. In 1992, it appears that the United States had substantial room for higher performance than many countries located closer to the equator.

Table 7.2
Relative performance across a sample of countries (deviations from mean of final residents)

Highest (+ 2 s.d.)	High (+ 1 s.d.)	Above average (0<s.d.<1)	Below average (-1<s.d.<0)	Low (-1 s.d.)	Lowest (-2 s.d.)
Aruba	Bahamas	Belgium	Algeria	Armenia	Estonia
Austria	Barbados	Burkina Faso	Australia	Czech Rep.	Hungary
Cayman Isl.	Costa Rica	Ecuador	Canada	E. Germany	Kiribati
Guam	Cyprus	Equat. Guinea	Dominica	Romania	Maldives
Israel	New Caledonia	Greece	Haiti	Solomon Is.	Tuvalu
Nauru	Singapore	Japan	Iraq	Russia	
Switzerland	West Germany	Mauritius	United States	Yugoslavia	

Source: Measured on 1992 income per capita (Parker 1997d).

For overall policy implications, the data clearly indicate that centralized regimes that limited economic liberties of their residents during the later half of the twentieth century drove these countries to the lowest levels on the filtered RPI.

Dynamics

Filtering does not reveal a theoretical limit or frontier to growth. One can use the filtered measures, however, to gauge likely growth dynamics. As optimal political strategies, information, technology, and knowledge diffuse around the world, countries near the frontier will grow slower than those far from the frontier. Among the next growth miracles, according to the filters, will likely be Armenia, Czech Republic, Slovakia, East Germany, North Korea, Romania, Russia, Yugoslavia (former republics), Estonia, Hungary, Latvia, and China. Countries likely to experience slower growth rates than these include Aruba, Austria, the Cayman Islands, Italy, Luxembourg, Switzerland, Costa Rica, West Germany, Brunei, Chad, Greece, and Singapore. Substantial growth is indicated for Canada, the United States, the United Kingdom, Mozambique, and Guinea Bissau (though to differing steady states).

The idea of filtering and using residuals is not completely satisfactory. Although it can surely be improved upon and be useful in terms of revealing likely dynamics and relative performance, the procedure lacks utility maximization and homeostatic comfort as a central notion. Supply-side effects may be confounded with homeostatic effects.

Idea 3: Using Local Performance Measures

Consumers maximize utility over a given time horizon. Completeness, then, requires that one consider two types of development measures: the time horizon and utilities derived from consumption. The former is directly a function of infant mortality and life expectancy. In the absence of unambiguous utility indicators, these capture a country's ability to satisfy the basic want of survival. As they are not homeostatic in nature, they represent the ultimate measures of human economic progress. It turns out that these indicators are gradually converging in absolute value to their biological limits across countries (see chapter 8). In the long run, marginal utilities derived from consumption will become the distinguishing measure of performance across countries.

For homeostatic consumption, the long-run problem will be establishing local and unambiguous measures of physical consumption required to establish human comfort. For food, these will minimally cover caloric, protein, and fat intake. Although the FAO has made great strides in this regard, additional work is required for transportation, energy, clothing, housing, and various forms of entertainment or leisure. Not until such standards are created will measures of consumption or income be useful in gauging relative performance. In relying more on real quantities consumed, the problem of convergence-divergence in prices across countries is also avoided to some extent (Dorwick and Quiggin 1997).

A partial step in this regard is found in the annual report to the U.S. Congress, by the State Department, covering human rights practices across some 200 countries.[7] In that report, acceptable work conditions and minimum wages are discussed. For some forty countries, the authors describe whether the worker earning minimum wages can maintain a "decent" standard of living for the family. This number is quite different from adjusting income for purchasing power parities as the basket of goods required may vary from country to country. Table 7.3 shows the annualized income estimated above which a decent standard of living is obtained for forty-one countries. The data indicate that this threshold varies in a similar fashion to income (the correlation is .88, $p\text{-}value<.0001$). The data imply that families earning less than \$21,000 in Denmark are less likely to have a decent standard of living compared to families earning \$1,500 in Gabon. Even if the figures are off by high percentages, they tend to confirm that comfort (i.e., decent living) is achieved at radically different levels of consumption across countries. The data further indicate that the variance in requisite consumption follows thermodynamic principles. Figure 7.4 shows that income required for a decent standard of living systematically varies with latitude ($R^2=.61$, $p\text{-}value<.0001$).

Table 7.3
Income to obtain decent standards of living

Country	Adequate income	Actual income	RPI	Latitude
Gabon	1320	4500	3.4	0
Central African Republic	182	440	2.4	4
Tanzania	347	260	0.8	4
Micronesia	2844	980	0.3	5
Liberia	576	430	0.7	6
Palau	5160	8800	1.7	7
Tuvalu	1956	556	0.3	8
Marshall Islands	4128	1500	0.4	10
Philippines	3096	860	0.3	11
Ethiopia	1000	130	0.1	12
Nicaragua	1586	754	0.5	12
Barbados	3006	7000	2.3	13
Samoa	972	900	0.9	14
Brazil	5328	2680	0.5	16
St. Kitts and Nevis	2904	4200	1.4	17
Haiti	7560	404	0.1	19
Mozambique	568	115	0.2	23
Oman	3120	6670	2.1	23
Taiwan	5879	10000	1.7	24
Botswana	1272	2769	2.2	24
Paraguay	2532	1545	0.6	25
Bahrain	3336	7800	2.3	26
Swaziland	360	1200	3.3	26
Bhutan	360	200	0.6	27
Nepal	293	179	0.6	27
Kuwait	9288	16400	1.8	29
Israel	8400	12100	1.4	32
Tunisia	1720	1820	1.1	36

Table 7.3 (continued)

Country	Adequate income	Actual income	RPI	Latitude
Malta	5424	7600	1.4	36
Japan	9900	26912	2.7	37
Greece	5796	8200	1.4	38
Portugal	4032	9000	2.2	39
Spain	5448	13200	2.4	40
New Zealand	7224	14900	2.1	41
Monaco	15912	16000	1.0	43
San Marino	14400	20000	1.4	44
France	13440	20414	1.5	46
Austria	14004	20192	1.4	47
Belgium	14568	19200	1.3	51
Netherlands	13656	18342	1.3	52
United Kingdom	12303	16702	1.4	53
Denmark	21312	24388	1.1	56

Source: Adapted from 1998 Country Reports on Human Rights, U.S. State Department.

From these, one can estimate a rough relative performance index by dividing actual per capita income by the income required for a decent standard of living. The higher this ratio, the more a country has been able to generate average incomes beyond minimal requirements for decent living conditions. The RPI reported in table 7.3 ignores the shape of income distributions within each country and does not adjust for family size (considering this would tend to inflate the RPI for most countries as income is measured on a per capita basis, whereas adequate income is generally established for a typical family of four persons). Figure 7.5 plots the RPI against latitude and shows that performance,

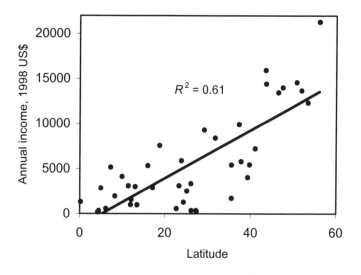

Figure 7.4
Annual income required to provide a decent standard of living across countries (adapted from 1998 Country Reports on Human Rights, U.S. State Department)

measured in this way, is strictly unrelated to latitude (R^2 *p-value*>.25). In other words, the *performance* of a country to meet the average decent consumption requirements for its population *is not determined by geographic disposition*. Rather, the requirements vary by geographic or thermodynamic disposition.

Table 7.3 does yield a few surprises, consistent with the statistical filtering suggested earlier. Some of the highest performing countries are African (e.g., Gabon). Within Europe, the highest performing countries are Portugal and Spain which are often seen as "poor" within the European Union based on the absolute level of average income per

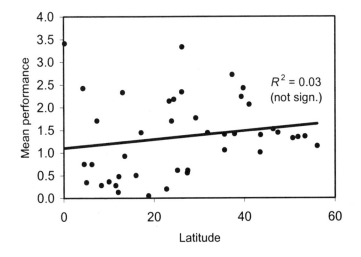

Figure 7.5
Relative performance (RPI) across countries and latitude (adapted from 1998 Country Reports on Human Rights, U.S. State Department)

capita. In fact, across the entire sample, income per capita is only marginally correlated to relative performance (.40; *p-value*<.02). Nevertheless, most of the countries failing to achieve average incomes to the level of adequate living standards are mostly concentrated toward the higher temperatures, or lower-income countries. This may be the result of there being few high-income countries in the sample. Though the data are suggestive, they indicate that absolute income per capita may, in the long run, be an inadequate or even misleading measure of relative economic progress when making such comparisons across countries spanning latitudes.

Clearly, far more precise measures of adequate consumption requirements across all countries and basket items are greatly needed. If such figures could be derived, then each country could be evaluated on the percentage of residents who have achieved this level of income-consumption. The effects of homeostatic utility differences should be explicitly incorporated into such measures and be established based on local physioeconomic conditions. These measures might be created by third parties, as local agencies often fail to report absolute measures of adequate consumption or standards below which a person is considered deprived of human dignity or comfort. Recently, the World Bank has stated that all persons should have an average income exceeding $1 per day. While this is a useful absolute lower end that might certainly apply globally, the World Bank and similar institutions should invest greater resources in estimating the real income required to maintain human decency in both high- and low-income countries. These should then be benchmarked across income distributions in each country. Abject poverty, whether in urban America or rural Somalia, remains abject wherever it may be located.

Idea 4: Direct Inspection

It is well known that if people are asked how satisfied they are with life, they will generally express equal satisfaction across wide income levels. If asked how much happier they would be with twice the income, many claim that their satisfaction with life would remain unchanged. People, it appears, have difficulty judging their potential utility under different income scenarios. Becker (1996, p. 11) takes exception with this view:

> It has been claimed for hundreds of years by philosophers, economists, and many others that most people undervalue future utilities because they have difficulty imagining the future. That may be true, but people train themselves to reduce and sometimes more than fully overcome any tendency toward undervaluation.

Without notions of cardinal utility, it is difficult to imagine how one might discover the utility equalizing level of income across any two individuals much less average residents across countries. If utility functions were identical and prices were international, then income would perfectly equate to realized utility.

Insurance companies, in practice, come close to dealing with this issue on a daily basis. Table 7.4 lists the average payouts for accidental deaths (normalized for the entire life of the resident) across a sample of European countries. These payouts will likely be highly correlated with the amounts required to maintain people in reasonable comfort during their life spans (i.e., the consumption value of a human life). Although the notion appears obtuse, private

Table 7.4
Insurance payouts based on the annuity value of a human life (1990)

Country	Value (k-ECU)	GNP/capita	Latitude
Greece	48	8,200	38
Portugal	78	9,000	39
Spain	100	13,200	40
France	269	20,414	46
United Kingdom	935	16,702	53
Denmark	628	24,388	56
Sweden	984	25,100	59
Finland	1,414	26,040	62

Source: Average payout levels for insurance claims; a multinational insurer.

insurers are faced with the valuation of life across countries (settling rates), which can be seen as a proxy for the amount that renders the survivors of a loss equally well off across countries (adjusting for policy size). These values would normally account for both basket effects and exchange rate distortions in costs of living. The estimates in Table 7.4 are reported by a private European insurer who has calculated such amounts for the year 1990.[8]

As indicated, the market value of human life varies across countries. The variances are large and strongly related to income ($R^2 = .67$; *p-value* < .01). The relationship to latitude, however, is far greater ($R^2 = .94$; *p-value* < .0001). These measures may suggest that residents across latitudes obtain similar marginal utilities at very different levels of annuity income.

An alternative to such aggregate data is to take Becker's notion of subjective utility assessment at face value. To explore this possibility, I have on various occasions implemented a variety of simple questionnaires that consistently point to the notion that marginal utilities can equate in line with the equatorial'paradox (or homeostatic preference variations). Such an approach is easily replicated for numerous measures of consumption (food, clothing, housing, electronic entertainment, etc.) or aggregate income provided that the respondents come from a sufficiently large sample spanning the world's latitudes. One such survey was conducted in an executive training course for the World Bank, jointly conducted by Harvard University, Stanford University, and the European Institute of Business Administration (INSEAD). Some of the participants were invited guests of the World Bank, including representatives from the Vatican, the International Monetary Fund, the World Resources Institute, and various private voluntary and nongovernmental organizations. The sample reported here consists of people from all of the world's continents who each have a keen professional interest in economic development, are generally trained as economists, and have extensively traveled in both low-income and high-income countries.

Each person was first asked to identify their country of origin: "What do you consider to be your country of origin?"

Two separate groups of sixty were then asked the following question:

> Assume that the average income of a German today is indexed at 100. Based on your knowledge, how much would the average person from your country of origin need to earn to be equally happy to the average German? Please base your answer on the index of 100 (e.g., if your country of origin is Germany, your answer must be 100; if the average person would be as happy as the average German by earning less, the answer must be between 0 and 100): _____

Variations on the term "happy", such as "satisfied with life" or "comfortable," generate similar results to those reported here. Likewise, one group was told to explicitly consider purchasing power parities, the other was given the question as stated above. The responses from the two groups follow the same pattern.

If households have similar utility functions for consumption items, the respondents would theoretically give a figure close to 100 percent (i.e., utility functions are roughly equivalent across countries). Although the sample sizes within each country are small and the approach is far from precise, the pattern that emerges supports the notion that marginals can equate at different levels of income or consumption. Table 7.5 reports the average response per

Table 7.5
Income required to generate equal utility to Germany, indexed at 100

Country	% Equal utility	Actual income	% of Germany	Latitude
Somalia	0	600	2.9	5
Mozambique	0	800	3.8	23
El Salvador	20	3,000	14.4	13
Georgia	20	1,570	7.5	41
Sudan	25	875	4.2	12
Egypt	30	4,400	21.2	28
Pakistan	30	2,600	12.5	29
Iran	30	5,500	26.4	33
Lebanon	30	4,400	21.2	34
China	30	3,460	16.6	35
Dominican Republic	33	4,700	22.6	19
Peru	34	4,420	21.3	10
India	34	1,600	7.7	21
Philippines	37	3,200	15.4	11
Bangladesh	38	1,330	6.4	23
Ethiopia	40	530	2.5	12
Mexico	50	7,700	37.0	24
Brazil	54	6,300	30.3	16
Ghana	55	2,000	9.6	7
Argentina	60	9,700	46.6	39
Spain	64	16,400	78.8	40
Canada	70	21,700	104.3	53
Netherlands	75	22,000	105.8	52
Ireland	78	18,600	89.4	52
Australia	80	21,400	102.9	28
Chile	80	11,600	55.8	36
Denmark	84	23,200	111.5	56
United Kingdom	95	21,200	101.9	53

Table 7.5 (continued)

Country	% Equal utility	Actual income	% of Germany	Latitude
Switzerland	97	23,800	114.4	46
United States	98	30,200	145.2	44
Germany	100	20,800	100.0	51
Japan	105	24,500	117.8	37
France	105	22,700	109.1	46
Norway	130	27,400	131.7	64

country, the income for each (1997 GNP per capita in ppp $), the percent that income represents vis-à-vis German income, and latitude.

In theory, the percent of equalization should be uncorrelated with income per capita (i.e., all responses should be equal to 100 or have random variance around this number). One finds, however, that correlation between the equalization percent and income per capita to be .92 (*p-value*<.0001). As Figure 7.6 indicates, the estimates provided are highly correlated to a country's latitude (the lower the latitude, the less a resident needs to consume to achieve equal utility to a German). If income is a direct measure of utility, then one would expect the line in figure 7.7 to fall horizontally flat at 100 percent. One can reject this hypothesis at *p-value*<.0001 as latitude explains some 54 percent of the variance across countries. Based on numerous replications of this question, this stylized fact appears to be robust to the type of respondents (e.g., development experts, government officials, economics

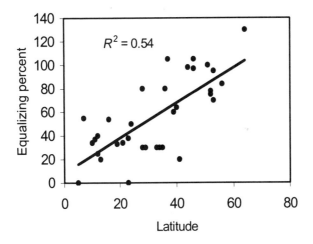

Figure 7.6
Income required to derive equal utility to Germans, across countries (percent, Germany = 100)

students, MBA students, and international relations students), and to the form of question asked (e.g., income, ppp-adjusted income, aggregate consumption, quantities of clothing, hours of watching television, hours of internet usage, etc.).[9]

In the case reported above, the figures caused a healthy debate among participants, with some accusing the representatives from Africa (especially Somalia and Mozambique who answered 0 percent) of not understanding the question. The economists from these countries, however, stood by their estimates. Even if we were to ignore these two low estimates, any answer substantially less or more than 100 is noteworthy. On the whole, the group rejected the notion that incomes need to equalize for countries to reach equal aggregate levels of satisfaction. This was perceived to be true for respondents residing in both the highest and lowest income countries (e.g., Norway needed more income than Germans to remain equally happy). Again, if the notion of income required to equalize utility can be made in a more objective and universally accepted manner, relative performance would be measured by the percent of each country's population achieving satisfactory levels of consumption (where marginal homeostatic utilities approach zero).

Summary

This chapter has made a few suggestions on how future research might account for differences in utility functions across countries, in line with physics-based physiology (the long-run source of the equatorial paradox). Far more work than that presented here will need to be devoted to this subject before adequate measures of relative performance can be accepted. The major conclusion from the data thus far presented is that high relative performance does not appear to be bounded by geographical considerations. Rather, countries with the lowest performance have tended to be those that have severely limited the freedoms of their residents from pursuing economic goals in hope of achieving greater levels of satisfaction or comfort (e.g., North Korea).

Furthermore, the use of aggregate or unadjusted measures of income or consumption may be misleading in revealing effective policy. Worse, low levels of these might mask highly successful policies (e.g., Costa Rica). In this regard, agencies active in development such as the World Bank, the United Nations Development Program, the International Monetary Fund, and various non-governmental organizations may have been incorrectly criticized as ineffective based on tainted measures. Similarly, high levels of income or consumption may lead to unjustified arrogance. Relying on raw measures tainted by the effects of homeostatic steady states will doom certain countries to the classification of "underdeveloped" when they, in fact, may have generated higher levels of relative economic performance than "developed" countries. The optimal hat in Finland is made of fur, in France a casquette, in Northern Mexican a sombrero, and in Brazil, for someone living under the Amazon canopy, nothing or perhaps a leaf. Just as development cannot be indicated by ranking countries based on their consumption values of hat types, neither can it be assessed by absolute values of food consumption, clothing consumption, housing consumption, energy consumption, or income per capita, which is largely comprised of these items.

Recent biomedical research, confirming Montesquieu's intuition, tends to indicate that this may also be true for a variety of purely psychological products (e.g., electronic or artificial entertainment, Prozac, and similar products or phototherapy). As a colleague from West Africa conjectured, a person who watches a lot of television in colder countries is considered normal. In warmer climates, the same person either has no friends or is psychologically unbalanced. If recent advances in neurobiology discussed in chapter 6 prove robust, people residing near the poles will crave and need to consume far more of these psychological items than those residing near the equator (e.g., due to luminosity-based differences in hypothalamic neurotransmitters or hormones) to achieve the same marginal psychological utility or homeostatic balance. Whether the craving for psychological balance can be achieved in the colder countries at high or low cost (work effort) remains an open question.

Notes

1.   Montesquieu (pp. 239–240).

2.   "U.S. to Buy Wheat" *International Herald Tribune*, July 20, 1998, p. 3.

3.   See Parker and Tavassoli (1999).

4.   World Resources Institute.

5.   See Rodriquez and Sachs (1999) for a discussion on how resources may actually slow growth.

6.   The data relied upon for items in this table are from Parker (1997d) and various issues of *European Marketing Data and Statistics*; *International Marketing Data and Statistics*, Euromonitor, 1996; and the United Nations statistical reports on caloric intake.

7. Former communist countries are excluded from this presentation given the lack of accounting for government-based subsidies. Inclusion of these does not change the basic outcome, but all of these countries appear as outliers.

8. Source: Average payout levels for insurance claims; a multinational insurer.

9. Conducted at INSEAD, the University of California, San Diego, the University of California, Los Angeles, MIT, Stanford University, and the Hong Kong University of Science and Technology.

8   Predictions

I was 90 percent wrong about Asia's future. The only consolation is that everyone else was 150 percent wrong.

—Paul Krugman[1]

Predicting economic growth is hazardous. In 1995, the Economist Intelligence Unit's predictions foresaw the fastest five-year growth economies to be concentrated in the Pacific Rim (Thailand, Singapore, Hong Kong, Korea, Indonesia, and Japan). Barro's (1997) empirical application of neoclassical growth models generated similar forecasts for these economies. Among the top twenty prospects for growth between the years 1996 and 2000, Barro (p. 44) forecasted 6.2 percent average annual growth for South Korea, 5.6 percent for the Philippines, 5 percent for Malaysia, 4.6 percent for Singapore, 4.6 percent for Thailand, and 4.2 percent for Hong Kong.[2] As the quotation above illustrates, poor predictions are quickly unmasked, sometimes on the front pages of the international press.

If short-run predictions are hazardous, it is not certain that long-run predictions will fair any better. With this in mind, this chapter will now consider the importance of various factors in explaining variances in long-run growth during the twenty-first century. These will cover the two central aspects of economic development: the length and the quality of life. The focus here will be mostly on the variances across countries and the degree to which β and σ convergence will occur. In the case of β convergence, certain absolute magnitudes can be foreseen.

Assumptions

Three working assumptions are used. First, no major changes in the world's environmental conditions are assumed. Though some global warming may take place, this will be far from the type of change needed to alter the forecasts provided.[3] Second, it is assumed that consumers will more freely maximize utility.[4] This assumption otherwise states that consumers will continue to strive for comfort and longevity, and that exogenous interference with this effort will decline over time. This assumption implies that the late-twentieth century trend toward market liberalization and democracy will generally continue, thus allowing firms, governments, and consumers to adopt optimal development strategies. Ever more efficient commercial institutions will continue to proliferate, as they have over the last 100 years, and firms will do their best to meet consumer needs with a requisite level of market power. Trends toward establishing a unique global currency, and rules of business conduct are assumed to continue. It is not unreasonable also to foresee the continual erosion of development path-dependencies by the diffusion of as yet unforeseen knowledge or technologies. These might be generated from private sources (seeking rents from intellectual property) or public sources (being supported by consumers hoping to benefit from public externalities). If one seeks to uncover factors that endogenize such invention (in a Schumpeterian sense), the distance between actual consumption and that required for long-lived homeostatic comfort may provide some of the answer (i.e., one is less likely to invent a cure for healthy people).

Finally, the third assumption is that longevity of oneself and one's offspring is a genetically hard-wired psychological need (i.e., we all seek to avoid entropy). Homeostatic consumption will definitely adhere to equation 3.5, or the first law of thermodynamics. As such, one assumes (or forecasts) that the conditional convergence observed in present-day consumption statistics will continue in the future according to physics-based physiological principles. In essence, one assumes that fundamental physical principles will not change during the next century. Here are forecasts, therefore, of the factors likely to explain divergences in consumption and relative performance in the long run. To bolster the notion that physioeconomics will dominate other explanations, we will focus on a few emphasized in academic and popular circles.

Prediction 1: Longevity Convergence with Consumption Divergence

The genetically determined life expectancy of humans is now believed to be somewhere around, but typically below, 120 years for virtually all persons (see Fogel 1994, pp. 383–384, for a review). The two key indicators of longevity are infant mortality and life expectancy which, across 161 countries, are highly correlated (-.95), as one might expect.[5] Despite income divergence over the last 250 years, the two key longevity measures have converged across countries to a low level.

As shown in chapter 2 (figures 2.5 and 2.6), there has been a long-run trend toward lower levels of infant mortality, beginning sometime after the nineteenth century germ theory of disease. Figure 8.1 shows the mean and standard deviations of infant mortality across 161 countries (calculated from data reported by the World Resources Institute 1998). For this measure one has an absolute theoretical bound (0/1000) to which the series can converge, but modern medicine generally achieves no better than 3/1000 births. At this low a level, ethical issues arise as many children are born with terminal or severe birth defects that are unrelated to the income of the parents or the state of technology. At 5 per 1000, this issue arises less frequently. The steady-state level of infant mortality was clearly above its long-run equilibrium dispersion in the nineteenth and twentieth centuries and is now approaching a historically low steady state (around 5 per

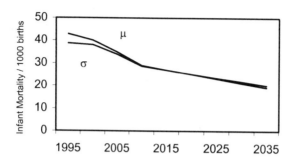

Figure 8.1
Infant mortality across 161 countries

1000 births) which will likely be achieved sometime toward the end of the twenty-first century. In the long run, therefore, variances in infant mortality will be unrelated to variances in consumption or income per capita.

The dynamics in life expectancy parallels that of infant mortality. Figure 8.2 shows the long-run dynamics of life expectancy across twenty-three high- and low-income countries for which historical series are available back to the nineteenth century.[6] A similar pattern to infant mortality is seen. Figure 8.3 indicates the mean dynamics and the dispersion over time for a period where a representative static sample applies. Large variances are seen in the eighteenth century and, by today's standards, very low levels of life expectancy in most places. In 1904, for example, the average life expectancy at birth in the United States was twenty-nine years for a black female and

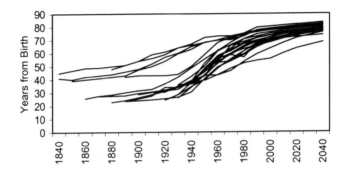

Figure 8.2
Life expectancy: 1840-2040

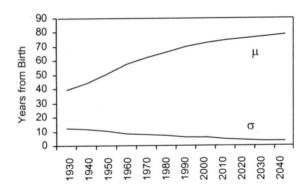

Figure 8.3
Life expectancy (twenty-three countries): 1930−2040

forty-nine years for a white female.[7] Life expectancies have since risen across all of the world's populations within and across countries.

Mean values appear to be asymptotically approaching a physiological limit of somewhere around 80 to 90 years. Though people living up to 122 years have been documented, the mean expectancy has remained constant since the 1960s in high-income countries. This plateau is observed even though these countries have experienced large increases in real income and heavily invested in health care technology. Although the poorer countries have lagged in this regard, one nevertheless observes a negative relationship between the convergence of this economic measure and that of income or consumption.

Figure 8.4 projects the mean and standard deviations of life expectancy across a broader sample of 184 countries (calculated from data reported by the World Resources Institute 1998). The dispersion level has been above its long-run steady state. Toward the end of the twenty-first century, the dispersion of life expectancies will approach a steady state near the theoretical limit of zero. Variances in life expectancy, therefore, will be unrelated to long-run variances in consumption or income per capita across countries.

Combined with infant mortality, the forecast for life expectancies paints a good picture for the world's future

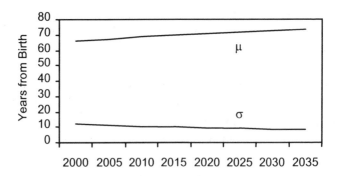

Figure 8.4
Life expectancy 184 countries: 2000 – 2035

with at least one aspect of the utility maximization problem: the consumer's time horizon. The twenty-first century discovery of cures or inexpensive treatments for the major diseases afflicting the tropics (e.g., malaria and AIDS) will accelerate this convergence. When longevity converges, then quality of life measures (e.g., comfort) will become the appropriate indicators of relative progress across countries.

Prediction 2: Literacy Convergence with Consumption Divergence

Literacy is often used as a proxy for accessibility to public knowledge or education. In addition to reflecting a certain quality of life, literacy is also cited as a factor influencing longevity; the knowledge required to improve infant and adult health need not involve capital intensive industry but can result from inexpensive knowledge transfer of

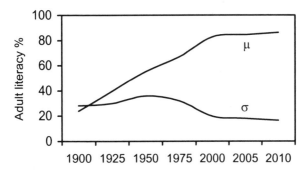

Figure 8.5
Literacy across 168 countries: 1900 to 2010

appropriate diet, hygiene, and dress. Literacy statistics are consistently available from the year 1900 and have been mostly estimated by religious missionaries.[8] Figure 8.5 indicates the average mean value and dispersion of literacy across 168 countries. Here again, a natural bound of 100 percent exists, and countries appear to be converging to this level. From 1900 to 1950, divergence in literacy was stable or increased slightly as the high-income countries outpaced the low-income countries, resulting in a gap.

Since the 1950s, means have continued to increase and dispersions have fallen. Provided governments make this a central theme of development, many low-income countries today have literacy levels that rival those of the more developed countries in the OECD. Examples include Costa Rica, Guyana, Uruguay, Thailand, and Surinam which all exceed 98 percent adult literacy. The global dynamics of literacy is all the more remarkable in that many peoples of the world have a mother tongue that derives from an oral tradition. Becoming literate for such populations typically requires learning a second language often of a colonial origin, or English, which has fundamentally different grammatical structures to native tongues. For these countries, literacy largely reflects the learning of a second language and sometimes a third language—a statistic that holds up well to certain developed nations, such as the United States, whose populations achieve literacy while remaining largely monolingual.

The historical record demonstrates an absolute convergence in literacy (toward 99 percent) and dispersions approaching zero sometime near the end of the twenty-first century. While progress needs to continue in the area of elementary and secondary schooling in most countries of the world, variances in literacy or measures of human capital based on literacy will be unrelated to long-run variances in consumption or income per capita.

Prediction 3: Population Growth Convergence with Consumption Divergence

In many models of growth, the dynamics of population is critical (Solow 1956). In the steady-state, population growth does not explain changes in standards of living. Changes (e.g., increases) in population growth rates, however, theoretically reduce the steady-state level of income-output per capita. Countries with high incomes per capita have low population growth rates. Indeed, cross-sectional data today indicate such a relationship, a fact often illustrated in macroeconomics textbooks (e.g., Mankiw 1997, p. 102–103).

Is this relationship persistent, or is it an artifact of the time frame considered? This question can be answered by considering the long-run variation of population growth rates to see if they are convergent. Population series extending back to the nineteenth century and projections of population growth into the twenty-first century appear to indicate that this relationship may be an artifact of the time frame considered, and the time frame when such a relationship will exist most is sometime in the latter half of the twentieth century, hence its inclusion in present-day textbooks.

Figure 8.6 shows the dynamics of population growth rates across the world's five major regions from 1700 to 2100: Africa, Asia, Europe, Latin America, and North America (adapted from Chesnais 1995, p. 50). Each of the major regions experienced a similar pattern of high growth rates followed by lower growth rates, sometimes interrupted by external shocks such as WWII. This dynamic was first observed in North America and last in Africa (growth rates having peaked and begun declining there over the last twenty years).

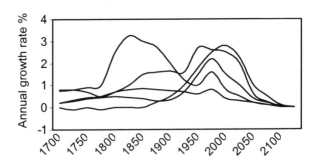

Figure 8.6
Population growth rates across regions: 1750 to 2100

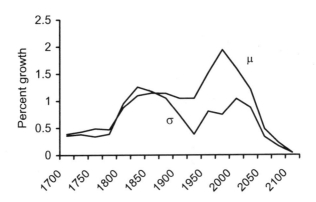

Figure 8.7
Mean and standard deviation of population growth rates in the five world regions

This pattern, studied at length in demography, is generated from the underlying dynamics of migration, fertility, mortality, and life expectancy. Figure 8.7 indicates that both means and variances of population growth rates have increased, then decreased across the five regions; both means and variances are estimated to converge to around zero sometime in the next century. Though estimates vary across sources, all point to a steady-state world population growth rate approaching zero sometime in the next 150 years or sooner. Based on the income data reported in Maddison (1995) and population growth rates given by Chesnais (1995), figure 8.8 shows the correlations between population growth rates and income per capita from 1750 to 2100 across the five regions. At the end points, the correlations logically approach zero. Before 1750, both incomes and population growth rates were largely convergent so as to prevent analysis of variance. In 2100, variance in population growth rates will also converge, so they will be unable to explain income or consumption variances. If one were to consider any time frame between 1750 and 1945, one would find only a weak, or even a strongly positive relationship between population growth rates and per capita income across countries — the opposite result to data collected after WWII.

Combined, the dynamics thus far illustrated lead to figure 8.9, which shows the aggregate world population levels from 1450 to 2100. Population growth rates remained low between 10,000 BC and the seventeenth century. Sometime during the eighteenth century, the world experienced

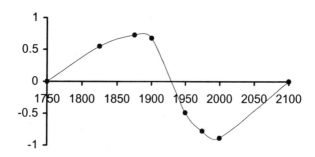

Figure 8.8
Correlation of population growth and income or consumption per
capita: 1750 to 2100

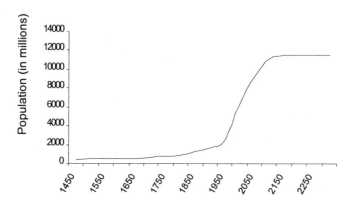

Figure 8.9
World population: A.D. 1450 to 2250

exponential growth. For this period, including today, population growth is associated with the size of population (see Kremer 1993). This relationship is foreseen to end sometime over the next 150 years as African population growth rates converge to those of high-income countries. Though some debate arises over the exact timing, most demographers foresee a stable population equilibrium sometime in the early twenty-second century at about 12 billion. At that point, all population growth rates, worldwide, are foreseen to converge to a similarly low level.

Underlying the aggregate dynamics are those of birth and fertility rates. Figures 8.10 to 8.13 show projected dynamics in the mean and standard deviations of the crude birth rate, the total fertility rate (births per woman), the net reproduction rate, and the average population growth rate, calculated from the World Resources Institute (1998) across 184 countries. Again, one sees that these measures of population dynamics will largely be convergent toward the end of the twenty-first century and will thus be unable to explain variances in consumption across countries.

Prediction 4: Migration Convergence and Consumption Divergence

As mentioned in chapter 2, a number of authors have noted the historical migration of populations from poor countries toward rich countries. The poorer people from low-income countries have historically migrated to become the poorer people (inexpensive labor) of high-income countries.

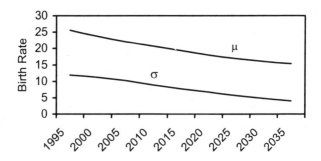

Figure 8.10
Birth rates dynamics (means and standard deviations): 1995 – 2040

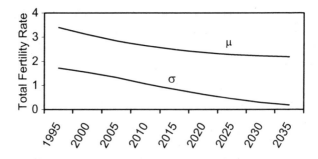

Figure 8.11
Fertility rate dynamics (means and standard deviations): 1995 – 2040

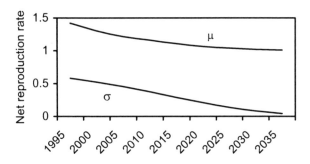

Figure 8.12
Net reproduction rates dynamics (means and standard deviations): 1995 –
2040

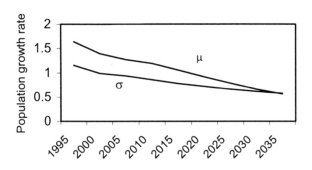

Figure 8.13
Population growth rate dynamics (means and standard deviations) 1995–
2040.

Although a number of factors have been used to explain this historical pattern, in the long run one would expect net migration levels to be unrelated to average consumption or incomes per capita across countries. Figure 8.14, calculated from data reported by the World Resources Institute (1998), projects an absolute convergence in net migration rates to zero, across 161 countries. As indicated, the mean and variance of net migration rates across countries will fall to zero sometime before the end of the twenty-first century.

Figure 8.14 is consistent with the notion that low-income countries will, on average, be able to achieve homeostatic comfort at lower levels of consumption. Seasonal migration (such as that seen by Germans during their holidays, or workers in agriculture) will surely persist. Massive migrations of the past, however, will eventually become exceptional events resulting less from economic disparities and more from exogenous and largely unforeseeable shocks (e.g., natural disasters, ethnic wars, etc.). By the end of the twenty-first century, dispersions in consumption will no longer be associated with net migration rates.

Prediction 5: Physioeconomic Factors Will Generate Most Variances in Long-Run Growth

The human consequences apparent in historical series raise important questions, not the least of which is "why are some countries so much more wealthy than others?" Combining the stylized facts in chapter 2 and the

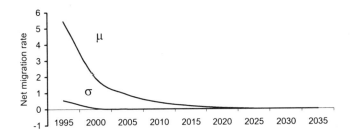

Figure 8.14
Net migration rates across 161 countries: 1995 – 2040.

predictions made above, it appears that long-run variances in growth will not likely be explained by variances in longevity, literacy, population dynamics, or migration as these are converging in the steady state to very narrow ranges. Similar forecasts can be made of political systems, economic institutions and business practices which are also converging. If not these factors, then what, in the long run, will explain variances in income or consumption?

Numerous academic fields have concentrated on answering this question, including sociology, demography, geography, history, development economics, and growth economics. The number and variety of explanations fills volumes as each almost represents a separate school of thought. Largely adequate reviews across various fields can be found in Barro and Sala-i-Martin (1995) who consider mostly neoclassical models of growth, Rostow (1990) who reviews classical models of growth, Landes

(1998) who considers economic history, Diamond (1997) who considers economic geography, Aghion and Howitt (1998) who consider Schumpetarian and endogenous models of growth, and Todaro (1997) who considers economic development paradigms. Even to the initiated, the variance in these explanations is astounding, to a point where it becomes difficult to believe that the various authors are addressing the same topic. Contrast, for example, the view espoused in Landes (1998, p. 475) in explaining the sources of wealth across the Asian tigers (i.e., Japan, Singapore, Taiwan, and Hong Kong):

> In all four the primary assets have been a work ethic that yields high product for low wages; and, as in Japan, an exceptional manual dexterity that comes from eating with chopsticks and is especially found in micro-assembly. This last argument brings smiles from my colleagues, but I stand by it. Much of modern assembly is fine tweezer work, and nothing prepares for it better than eating with chopsticks from early childhood.

This view contrasts with that of Dornbusch et al. (1998, p. 64):

> The fact remains that the tigers have achieved something extraordinary in human history... It is reassuring to see that this can be done the old-fashioned way, through saving, hard work, and competition.

In addition to using different explanatory variables, it is frequently observed that one school uses the other school's dependent variable as an independent variable and vice versa (e.g., starting conditions in income drive education variances; starting conditions in education drive changes in income; similarly for fertility, population growth rates, corruption, etc.). Simultaneity problems aside, if one accepts a school's explanation as primal, one must also accept that others suffer from gross specification errors and, perhaps, spurious inference.

What often matters is not what people say, but what they believe. To gauge perceptions, the 120 executives of the World Bank training seminar mentioned in chapter 7 responded to the following question:

> Incomes per capita vary substantially across the world's 200+ countries; from about $500 to some $40,000. What factors explain this variance? Based on your knowledge, please allocate 100 percentage points across the following factors to explain this variance. Do so for three periods in time: the years 1900, 1998 and 2050.

Each of the items listed reflect particular schools of thought that have emerged to explain cross-country variances over the last two centuries of economic thinking. They are presented by rough order of exogeneity (climate and terrain being the most exogenous). A category "other" was included but only one participant filled in this option and allocated 3 percent to "health care." The variances of responses are roughly proportional to the mean values. Mean response values are indicated in table 8.1; sums exceed 100 due to rounding.

Several patterns emerge from these perceptions. Above all, the respondents believe that the explanatory model is not stable over time. At the turn of the century, economic geography is seen as dominating growth with natural resources and strategic location accounting for 40 percent of the explained variance. Contrary to authors who have recently emphasized geographic explanations (e.g., Sachs, Krugman, Landes and Diamond), natural resources and strategic location were seen as explaining only 18 percent in 1998 and will fall to 12 percent in 2050. Cultural and political institutions also show declines from 19 to 16 percent over the 150-year period considered. Economic, business, and social factors are seen as having more influence over time, growing from 29 to 39 percent. Economic policies alone are seen to explain only 16 percent of variance. This view concords with the generally held view that "fine tuning" generally does not alter steady state paths, as noted by Barro and Sala-i-Martin (1995, p. 4−5).

Table 8.1
Perceived explained variances across development paradigms

	1900	1998	2050
Natural resources (e.g., climate, terrain, mineral and marine resources)	24	11	8
Strategic location (e.g., with a natural harbor along a trade route)	16	7	4
Cultural institutions (e.g., religious, linguistic, artistic)	8	6	6
Political institutions (e.g., democracy, monarchy, dictatorship, theocracy)	11	12	10
Economic policies (e.g., monetary/fiscal, liberal versus managed)	11	16	17
Business climate (e.g., corruption levels, commercial traditions/codes)	10	13	12
Social climate (e.g., crime/law enforcement, ethnic tensions, gender roles)	8	10	10
Knowledge (e.g., human capital, technology, expertise, education)	15	25	36
Total	103	100	103

The biggest gain taken from economic geography is "knowledge" which is seen to explain only 15 percent of variances observed in 1900, but will increase to become the single most important factor reaching 36 percent in 2050 (though the variance on this question was the highest). In general, the perception is that exogenous factors will eventually explain less of economic development variations, while endogenous factors will dominate the next century. It is not surprising, therefore, to see the recent strategy of the World Bank to become a "knowledge bank."

If one accepts absolute latitude to be natural resource (driving homeostatic physiology and long-run steady states), then the previous chapters would indicate the following forecasts of explained variances:

	2050	2100
Natural resources	70	80
Strategic location	5	5
Cultural institutions	5	3
Political institutions	5	5
Economic policies	5	1
Business climate	5	5
Knowledge	5	1
Total	100	100

A simple comparison of this forecast to that of the experts in table 8.1 reveals almost orthogonal distributions. The most striking difference between the two is the belief that knowledge will play an important role in explaining variances in the future, versus exogenous physioeconomic factors, largely driven by latitude-based thermodynamics. This forecast does not downplay the numerous social, political, and cultural factors previously identified in the literature (e.g., gender roles, racism, or corruption). It simply foresees that the more important impediments to growth will be lifted and those encouraging growth to be universally implemented. Since the adoption of liberal political and economic institutions will converge in the long run; these will not be able, therefore, to explain long-run variations in the steady state.

Earlier, it was shown why thermodynamics might affect growth but it has not been discussed why knowledge will not. Literacy will certainly become more general as time progresses. While literacy improves the transference of knowledge, it does not speak to the quality of knowledge. The forecast above is based on the principle that accurate (i.e., high quality) knowledge is virtually costless, not only because much of it falls in the public domain but also that firms will compete away its profit so that prices approach marginal costs (which is close to zero and can thus be easily acquired by all).

To make this point, an intuitive analytic argument will be used.[9] Figure 8.14 considers two firms selling knowledge, say, in the form of consulting reports or raw information. In the case where both firms sell extremely accurate information and offer the same perspective (e.g., a scientific methodology), the buyer will only purchase one report.

The two firms engage in severe, or Bertrand-like, price competition. The price of accurate scientific knowledge is driven to marginal costs. This explains why basic science is inexpensive to acquire. Scientists have similar perspectives and they sell relatively accurate information. One scientist is a substitute for another.

Now consider the case where the user wishes to invest in China and needs a ten-year forecast of consumer demand for, say, lumber. The manager is approached by two consulting firms. This time, the suppliers have very different perspectives; one firm builds up demand forecasts by considering trends in housing and family structure, while the other considers time series of trade data. In this case, the manager will end up purchasing both reports and the two firms charge high prices. Since the data sold are forecasts, they tend to be inaccurate. The user of the information will combine the two information sources prior to making a decision; the firms sell Cournot complements. In this case, information is both costly and inaccurate. Not because the suppliers are incompetent, but because they are advising on uncertain events. This explains why management consultants are paid far more than accountants, for example, even though the accountants are more accurate than the consultants in the information they sell.

If one defines knowledge to be accurate or nonspeculative information, it will be inexpensive in the long run as firms

	Sellers have different perspectives	Sellers have same perspective
Buyer faces high uncertainty (inaccurate data)	Buys two reports Complements high profit & prices	Buys one to two reports
Buyer faces low uncertainty (accurate data)	Buys one to two reports	Buys one report Substitutes low profit & prices

Figure 8.15
Competition in information or knowledge markets (adapted from Sarvary and Parker 1997)

compete away profits. Objective knowledge, therefore, will not be a barrier to, nor a factor likely to explain variances in, long-run growth. High-income countries will not be "informed" and low-income countries will not be "ignorant." Growth in consumption will largely be based on each country's willingness to let their citizens exploit knowledge and not on the level of knowledge in each. Hence, the forecast given above places a certain percent on economic and business considerations that might allow for the creation and/or exploitation of knowledge. Although knowledge or technology asymmetries across countries can surely affect variances, these are foreseen to decrease over time, or be of local relevance (e.g., residents of the United

States will know better how to produce internal heating systems in the long run, but this knowledge will be irrelevant to residents living toward the equator).

Summary

A central question to international planners is whether a specific country will experience rapid or slow growth in the long-run. It is useful to distinguish between two types of development indicators: longevity and consumption. In the case of longevity, highest growth will occur in countries where current knowledge, technology, or institutions have been unable to eradicate major diseases or transfer best practice. Highest future growth for longevity, therefore, will mostly occur in countries in the topics or those, like North Korea, that have implemented repressive policies. If utility realization is a key concept to development, then longevity convergence (toward universal biological limits) cannot be anything but the most important goal for international development investments and intellectual endeavor. Investments in medical research, safe drinking water, pre-natal care, general healthcare and education, across both genders, have thus far proven most beneficial in this regard.

With respect to consumption, as discussed in chapter 7, the general prediction here is that high consumption growth will occur in countries that are now farthest from their steady states (mostly concentrated in former communist countries, especially in the higher latitudes). In this case, the country that will experience the highest absolute growth over the next century will be North Korea. This forecast assumes that the North Korean government will allow its residents to reach their steady-state levels of consumption in food, clothing, housing, and entertainment. At currently $900 ppp-income per capita, North Korea will grow to somewhere around $30,000 income per capita, in current dollars. This will occur some twenty to fifty years after its economy is liberalized (a time frame consistent with the empirical demonstration of post-war European economies converging to the United States). Similar growth will occur in Poland, or Russia (converging to western Europe or the United States), for example, and in northern China along the Shanghai-Beijing corridor (converging to Japan or the United States).

Table 8.2 summarizes global forecasts across various measures of longevity and quality of life. Overall, the vision is rather optimistic for the next century. Within 100 years, people the world over will live equally long lives (or at least with minor dispersions around a high mean). Disparities in progress will therefore be measured in quality of life, or comfort and not longevity. To achieve the same level of comfort, consumption will vary for most basket items in line with the equatorial paradox. This will be true even if all countries of the world, for whatever reason, reach the same level of income per capita. Experience has shown that comfortable standards of living can be achieved in low-consumption countries. High relative performance in achieving decent living standards

Table 8.2
Long-run forecasts across development indicators: 2100

Indicator	β	μ	σ
Longevity			
Infant mortality	Yes	≤4/1000	≅ 0
Life expectancy	Yes	<90 years	≅ 0
Demography			
Fertility	Yes	≅ 2	≅ 0
Birth rate	Yes	≅ 10	≅ 0
Death rate	Yes	≅ 10	≅ 0
Population growth	Yes	≅ 0	≅ 0
Net migration	Yes	≅ 0	≅ 0
Net reproduction rate	Yes	≅ 1	≅ 0
Rate of natural increase	Yes	<1	≅ 0
Population growth	Yes	≅ 0	≅ 0
Education			
Adult literacy	Yes	≅ 99%	≅ 0
Political indicators			
Communism (1=yes)	Yes	0	≅ 0
Democracy (1=yes)	Yes	1	≅ 0
Consumption per capita			
GDP/capita	No	n.a.	n.a.
Food intake	No	2500 cal./day	≈500
Climate			
Latitude	No	25	17

will not be bounded by geographic considerations, if performance is measured as distance to comfort-achieving, steady-state consumption. The use of income per capita as a universally applicable measure of performance should end. Rather, disaggregate measures with local applicability should dominate discussions of economic well-being and performance.

Nothing dictates an absolute consumption or income frontier for any given location for nonphysiological consumption (e.g., entertainment, the current satisfaction derived from savings for current or future generations, leisure or philanthropy). One can only speculate that the ultimate limit to average income will be driven by cravings for these items. If the primary goal in life is to achieve both physiological and psychological balance (homeostasis), then some limit must exist. The amount of work one is willing to devote to achieving this balance, however, will always be limited. In general, the less work the better. In this regard, full development might only be achieved when work is indistinguishable from entertainment, and that only a few hours are required per year to meet homeostatic needs. To this end, productivity-enhancing technological progress observed to date is rather rudimentary, at best.

Who, in the long run, will need to consume more to reach steady-state equilibrium? Montesquieu makes the last forecast presented:

> There is a kind of balance in Europe between the
> nations of the South and the North. The first have
> all sorts of the comforts of life and few needs; the
> second have many needs and few of the comforts
> of life. In the former, nature has given much and
> they ask but little of it; to the others nature gives
> little, and they ask much of it. Equilibrium is
> maintained by the [comfort] it has given to the
> southern nations and by the industry and activity it
> has given to those of the north. The later are
> obliged to work much; if they did not, they would
> lack everything and become barbarians.[10]

Ultimate Predictions

Physics has the upper hand when it comes to predicting the
very long run. It is known that the universe comes to an
end when all of the protons and neutrons, the things
everything is made of, will ultimately decay into leptons
some 10^{31} years from now. Well before then, or in about 10
billion years, the sun and all life in our solar system will
become extinct. Assuming we are nothing special
compared to other species, then much sooner than that,
using the Copernican principle of species longevity, some
have calculated that the humans of today will become
extinct sometime between 5,000 and 7.8 million years from
now.[11] During that period, there is a nonnegligible
probability that the earth will undergo major climatic
change (man-made or not), or experience a species

eradicating calamity graphically illustrated in science-fiction thrillers. Sooner yet, Keynes tells us that in less than 100 years, the reader will be dead. The second law of thermodynamics, alas, always gets its way. Physics alone, however, can not reveal the optimal form of political economy nor the best policies to ensure that we all get the best out of our short lives, wherever we may live. The same might be said for economics, alone.

Notes

1. *International Herald Tribune*, March 26, 1998, p. 11.

2. At the time of this writing, certain of these Asian economies are coming out of their deepest recessions since WWII, with most recording negative growth rates over the last two years.

3. A number of authors have considered the impact of growth on the environment. Grossman and Krueger (1995), for example, show little relationship between growth and permanent changes to the environment.

4. The general form is to maximize the integral of discounted utility ($e^{-\rho t}$), from 0 to T of U(X), subject to $PX \leq Y$, where T is the consumers' life span, discounted by a time preference constant ρ, for a vector of consumption levels X. The consumer is constrained to self-generated income (or inherited wealth) Y, and the vector of prices P. Although studies of growth have focused great attention on the constraint (Y, and P), the objective function clearly make time, T, a key element. A person's premature death, for all reasonable values of ρ, is economically catastrophic; this is especially true if one expands the definition of X to a variety of consumption items with low explicit or implicit prices (e.g., friends, family, the environment, conversation, etc.). The variables

most affecting this aspect of the problem are clearly infant mortality and life expectancy.

5.   Based on simple correlation; source: World Bank, *World Development Indicators*, 1998.

6.   Collected from various national agencies.

7.   U.S. Department of Commerce, Bureau of the Census, *Statistical Abstracts of the United States*, 1989, p. B99—115.

8.   See the impressive work of Barrett (1982) whose figures have been augmented by those given by the World Resources Institute (1998) for this paragraph.

9.   See Sarvary and Parker (1997).

10.   Montesquieu (p. 355).

11.   Malcom W. Browne, "The Limits of Existence: Just Assume we're Nothing Special," *International Herald Tribune*, June 3, 1993, p. 5.

References

Ades, Alberto, and Hak B. Chua. 1997. "Thy Neighbor's Curse: Regional Instability and Economic Growth." *Journal of Economic Growth* 2 (September): 279–304.

Adler, Frederick R. 1998. *Modeling the Dynamics of Life.* Pacific Grove: Brooks/Cole Publishing Company.

Aghion, Philippe, and Peter Howitt. 1998. *Endogenous Growth Theory.* Cambridge, MA: The MIT Press.

Alexandrinus, Hero of 100 B.C. In Robert Fludd, *Utriusque Cosmi Historia,* 1617, Oppenheim: 30–33. Reprinted in Benzinger, Theodor H. ed. 1977. *Temperature: Part I. Arts and Concepts.* Benchmark Papers in Human Physiology. vol. 10. Stroudsburg, PA: Dowden, Hutchinson & Ross: 22–29.

Andersson, B., R. Grant, and S. Larsson. 1956. "Central Control of Heat Loss Mechanisms in the Goat." *Acta Physiologica Scandinavica* 37: 261.

Anselin, Luc. 1988. *Spatial Econometrics: Methods and Models.* Dordrecht: Kluwer Academic Publishers.

Armstrong, H.W. 1995. "An Appraisal of the Evidence from Cross-Sectional Analysis of the Regional Growth Process Within the European Union." In *Convergence and Divergence Among European Regions*. H.W. Armstrong, and R.W. Vickerman, eds. *European Research in Regional Science* 5: 66—68.

Aronsohn, Eduard, and Julius Sachs. 1885. "Die Beziehungungen des Gehirns zur Korperwarme und zum Fieber." Pflueger's Archive, European Journal of Physiology. 37: 232—249, 270—282, 288—300. Summarized in English in Benzinger, Theodor H. ed. 1977. *Temperature: Part II. Thermal Homeostasis.* Benchmark Papers in Human Physiology. vol. 10. Stroudsburg, PA: Dowden, Hutchinson & Ross: 54—56.

Azariadis, Costas. 1996. "The Economics of Poverty Traps. Part One: Complete Markets." *Journal of Economic Growth* 1,4 (December): 421—448.

Bairoch, Paul. 1981. "The Main Trends in National Economic Disparities Since the Industrial Revolution." In Bairoch and Levy-Leboyer, eds. *Disparities in Economic Development.* London: Macmillan.

Barbour, Henry Gray. 1912. "Die Wirkung unmittelbarer Ermarmung und Abkuhlung der Warmezentra auf die Korperperatur." *Archives of Experimental Pathology and Pharmacology.* 70:1.

Barrett, David B. 1982. *World Christian Encyclopedia: A Comparative Study of Churches and Religions in the Modern World, AD 1900 – 2000.* New York: Oxford University Press.

Barro, Robert J. 1997. *Determinants of Economic Growth: A Cross-Country Empirical Study.* Cambridge, MA: The MIT Press.

Barro, Robert J. 1989. "An Efficiency-Wage Theory of the Weather." *Journal of Political Economy* 97, 4: 999 – 1001.

Barro, Robert J. 1996. "Democracy and Growth." *Journal of Economic Growth* 1, 1 (March): 1 – 28.

Barro, Robert J. and Xavier Sala-i-Martin. 1992, "Convergence." *Journal of Political Economy* 2: 223 – 436.

Barro, Robert J., and Xavier Sala-i-Martin. 1995. *Economic Growth.* New York: McGraw-Hill.

Barro, Robert J., and Xavier Sala-i-Martin. 1997. "Technological Diffusion, Convergence, and Growth." *Journal of Economic Growth* 2, 1 (March): 1 – 26.

Basu, Susanto, and David N. Weil. 1998. "Appropriate Technology and Growth." *The Quarterly Journal of Economics* CXIII, 4 (November): 1025 – 1054.

Baumol, William J. 1986. "Productivity Growth, Convergence and Welfare: What the Long-Run Data Show?" *American Economic Review* 76 (December): 1072 – 1085.

Becker, Gary S. 1981. *A Treatise on the Family*. Cambridge, MA: Harvard University Press.

Becker, Gary S. 1993. "Nobel Lecture: The Economic Way of Looking at Behavior." *Journal of Political Economy* 101, 3: 385−409.

Becker, Gary S. 1996. *Accounting for Tastes*. Cambridge, MA: Harvard University Press.

Ben-David, Dan, and Michael B. Loewy. 1998. "Free Trade, Growth, and Convergence." *Journal of Economic Growth* 3, 2 (June): 143−170.

Durham, J. Benson 1999, "Economic Growth and Political Regimes," *Journal of Economic Growth* 4 (March): 81−111.

Benzinger, T.H. 1967. "The Thermal Homeostasis in Man." In Benzinger, Theodor H. ed. 1977. *Temperature: Part II. Thermal Homeostasis.* Benchmark Papers in Human Physiology. vol. 10. Stroudsburg, PA: Dowden, Hutchinson & Ross: 289−377.

Benzinger, Theodor H. ed. 1977a. *Temperature: Part I. Arts and Concepts*. Benchmark Papers in Human Physiology. vol. 10. Stroudsburg, PA: Dowden, Hutchinson & Ross.

Benzinger, Theodor H. ed. 1977b. *Temperature: Part II. Thermal Homeostasis.* Benchmark Papers in Human Physiology. vol. 10. Stroudsburg, PA: Dowden, Hutchinson & Ross.

Bernard, Claude. 1876. *Lecons sur la Chaleur Animale.* Paris: 121, 123–139. Reprinted in Benzinger, Theodor H. ed. 1977. *Temperature: Part I. Arts and Concepts.* Benchmark Papers in Human Physiology. vol. 10. Stroudsburg, PA: Dowden, Hutchinson & Ross: 229–250.

Birchenhall, C.R., R.C. Blanden-Hovell, A.P.L. Chui, Denise R. Osborn, and J.P. Smith, "A Seasonal Model of Consumption." *The Economic Journal* 99 (September): 837–843.

Blaxter, Kenneth. 1989. *Energy Metabolism in Animals and Man.* Cambridge: Cambridge University Press.

Blessing, William W. 1997. *The Lower Brainstem and Bodily Homeostasis.* Oxford: Oxford University Press.

Bligh, J., and K. Voigt. 1990. *Thermoreception and Temperature Regulation.* Berlin: Springer-Verlag.

Bloom, F.E., A. Lazerson, and L. Hofstadter. 1985. *Brain, Mind and Behavior.* New York: W.D. Freeman.

Boerhaave, Hermannus. 1709. Elementa Chemiae. Leiden, 1732: 364–366. Reprinted in Benzinger, Theodor H. ed. 1977. *Temperature: Part I. Arts and Concepts.* Benchmark Papers in Human Physiology. vol. 10. Stroudsburg, Pennsylvania: Dowden, Hutchinson & Ross, Inc.: 106–115.

Brenner, Barry M., and Jay H. Stein eds. 1987. *Body Fluid Homeostasis.* In Contemporary Issues in Nephrology. New York: Churchill Livingstone.

Brown, R.E. 1994. *Introduction to Neuroendocrinology.* Cambridge: Cambridge University Press.

Burton, A.C., and Edholm, O.G. 1955. "The Thermal Insulation of the Air." In *Man in a Cold Environment*: 47–72.

Cambell, D.J., and C. Katz, 1975. *Atlas of the Least Developed Nations: Groups and Characteristics.* Worcester, MA: Clark University.

Carlson, Neil R. 1981. *Physiology of Behavior.* 2d. ed. Boston: Allyn & Bacon Inc.

Carpenter, R.H.S. 1996. *Neurophysiology.* 3d ed. New York: Oxford University Press.

Caselli, Francesco, Gerardo Esquivel, and Fernando Lefort. 1996. "Reopening the Convergence Debate: A New Look at Cross-Country Growth Empirics." *Journal of Economic Growth* 1, 3 (September): 363–389.

Cena, K., and J.A. Clark. 1979. "Transfer of Heat Through Animal Coats and Clothing." *International Review of Physiology*, Environmental Physiology III 20: 1–42.

Chesnais, Jean-Claude. 1995. *La Démographie.* Paris: Presses Universitaires de France.

Chiras, Daniel D. 1999. *Human Biology: Health, Homeostasis, and the Environment.* New York: Jones & Barlett Publishing.

Cigno, Alessandro, 1981. "Growth with Exhaustible Resources and Endogenous Population." *Review of Economic Studies* XLVIII: 281 – 287.

Clark, R.P., and O.G. Edholm. 1985. *Man and His Thermal Environment*. London: Edward Arnold.

Cohen, Daniel. 1996. "Tests of the 'Convergence Hypothesis': Some Further Results." *Journal of Economic Growth* 1, 3 (September): 351 – 361.

Cooper, K., P. Lomax, E. Schonbaum, and W.L. Veale. 1986. *Homeostasis and Thermal Stress: Experimental and Therapeutic Advances*. 6th International Symposium on the Pharmacology of Thermoregulation, Jasper, Alta., 1985. Basel: Karger.

Crafts, N.F.R. 1985. *The Conditions of Economic Progress*. London: Macmillan.

Darwin, Charles. 1859. *On the Origin of Species*. London: British Museum (Natural History).

DeLong, J. Bradford, and Lawrence H. Summers. 1991. "Equipment Investment and Economic Growth." *Quarterly Journal of Economics* 106, 2 (May): 445-502.

De Medici, Leopoldo. 1667. Saggi di Naturali Esperienze fatti nell'Academiaa del Cimento, Florence: 1 – 5, 7, 9 – 11. Reprinted in Benzinger, Theodor H. ed. 1977. *Temperature: Part I. Arts and Concepts*. Benchmark Papers in Human

Physiology. vol. 10. Stroudsburg, PA: Dowden, Hutchinson & Ross, Inc.: 56−73.

Diamond, Jared. 1997. *Guns, Germs, and Steel*. New York: W.W. Norton & Company.

Donovan, B. T. 1985. *Hormones and Human Behavior*. Cambridge: Cambridge University Press.

Dornbusch, Rudiger, Stanley Fischer, and Richard Startz. 1998. *Macroeconomics*. 7th ed. New York: Irwin/McGraw-Hill.

Dorwick, Steve, and John Quiggin. 1997. "True Measures of GDP Convergence." *The American Economic Review* (March): 41−64.

Durand, Jacques, and Jeanne Raynaud. 1979. *Thermal Comfort: Physiological and Psychological Bases*, Paris: INSERM.

Durham, J. Benson. 1999 "Economic Growth and Political Regimes." *Journal of Economic Growth* 4, 1 (March): 81-111.

Ericksen, Jerald L. 1998. *Introduction to the Thermodynamics of Solids*. Applied Mathematics Sciences, vol. 131. New York: Spinger-Verlag.

Euler, Curt von. 1950. "Slow Temperature Potentials in the Hypothalamus." *Journal of Cellular Comp. Physiology* 36: 333.

Evans, Paul. 1996. "Using Cross-Country Variances to Evaluate Growth Theories." *Journal of Economic Dynamics and Control* 20: 1027–1049.

Evans, P., and G. Karras. 1993. "Do Standards of Living Converge?" *Economic Letters* 43: 146–155.

Fanger, P.O. 1977. "Thermal Discomfort Caused by Radiant Asymmetry, Local Air Velocities, Warm or Cold Floors, and Vertical Air Temperature Gradients." *Thermal Comfort*, Jacques Durand, and Jeanne Raynaud eds. INSERM, December, 75: 145–152.

Farenheit, Daniel Gabriel. 1724. "Experiments Made on the Degree of Warmth of Some Boiling Liquids." Philosphical Transcripts of the Royal Society, London, 33 (381): 1–3 (1724–1725). Reprinted in Benzinger, Theodor H. ed. 1977. *Temperature: Part I. Arts and Concepts.* Benchmark Papers in Human Physiology. vol. 10. Stroudsburg, PA: Dowden, Hutchinson & Ross: 83–93.

Feynman, Richard P., Robert B. Leighton, and Matthew Sands. 1963. *The Feynman Lectures on Physics.* vol. 1. Reading, MA: Addison-Wesley Publishing Company.

Fogel, Robert W. 1994. "Economic Growth, Population Theory, and Physiology: The Bearing of Long-Term Processes on the Making of Economic Policy." *American Economic Review* 84, 3 (April): 369–395.

Folinsbee, Lawrence J., Jeames A. Wagner, Julian F. Borgia, Barbara L. Drinkwater, Jeffrey A. Gliner, and John F. Bedi.

eds. 1978. *Environmental Stress: Individual Human Adaptations*. New York: Academic Press.

Folk, G. Edgar. 1974. *Environmental Physiology*. 2d ed. Philadelphia: Lea & Febiger.

Folk, G. Edgar, Mariv L. Riedesel, and Diana L. Thrift. 1998. *Princliples of Integrative Environmental Physiology*. San Francisco: Autin & Winfield Publishers.

Food and Agriculture Organization of the United Nations. 1974. *Handbook on Human Nutritional Requirements*. Rome: FOA.

Food and Agriculture Organization of the United Nations. 1996. *The Sixth World Food Survey*. Rome: FOA.

Food and Nutrition Board. 1989. *Recommended Daily Allowances, 1989 revision*. Washington, D.C.: National Academie of Sciences–National Research Council.

Fox, R.H., Z. Even-Paz, P.M. Woodward, and J.M. Jack. 1973. "A Study of Temperature Regulation in Yemenite and Kurdish Jews in Israel." *Philosophical Transactions of the Royal Society of London Series B* 226: 149−68.

Franklin, Benjamin. 1758. Letter XXXII to Dr. L of Charles-Town, South Carolina. In Experiments and Observation on Electricity, 5th ed. London, 1774: 371−376. Reprinted in Benzinger, Theodor H. ed. 1977. *Temperature: Part I. Arts and Concepts*. Benchmark Papers in Human Physiology. vol.

10. Stroudsburg, PA: Dowden, Hutchinson & Ross: 200 – 205.

Fries, James F. "The Compression of Morbidity: Near or Far?" *Milbank Quarterly* 67, 2: 208 – 32.

Gagge, A.P., Y. Nishi, and R.G. Nevins. 1976. "The Role of Clothing in Meeting Federal Energy Agency Energy Conservation Guidelines." *ASHRAE Transactions* 82(II): 234.

Galbraith, John Kenneth. 1951. "Conditions for Economic Change in Underdeveloped Countries." *Journal of Farm Economics* 33 (November).

Galbraith, John Kenneth. 1979. *The Nature of Mass Poverty.* Cambridge, MA: Harvard University Press.

Galilei, Galileo. 1603. *Operer di Galileo Galilei*, vol. VII, A. Favaro, ed. Florence (1890-1909): 377, 634 – 635. Reprinted in Benzinger, Theodor H. ed. 1977. *Temperature: Part I. Arts and Concepts.* Benchmark Papers in Human Physiology. Vol. 10. Stroudsburg, PA: Dowden, Hutchinson & Ross: 30 – 33.

Galor, Oded, and Daniel Tsiddon. 1997. "The Distribution of Human Capital and Economic Growth." *Journal of Economic Growth* 2, 1 (March): 93 – 124.

Garry, R.D., R. Passmore, G.M. Warnock, and J.V.G.A. Durnin. 1955. *Studies on the Expenditure of Energy and the Consumption of Food by Miners and Clerks, Fife Scotland.*

Special report series no. 289. Medical Research Council. London: H.M.S.0.

Gartmann, Heinz. 1957. *Man Unlimited: Technological Challenge to Human Endurance.* Translated from the German by Richard and Clara Winston. London: Jonathan Cape.

Gershenkron, A. 1962. *Economic Backwardness in Historical Perspective.* New York: Praeger.

Giancoli, Douglas C. 1989. *Physics for Scientists and Engineers,* 2d ed. New Jersey: Prentice Hall: 497.

Goldman, Ralph F. 1977. "The Role of Clothing in Modifying the Human Thermal Comfort Range." *Thermal Comfort,* INSERM, 75: 163 – 176.

Gottlieb, R. 1890. *Archives of Experimental Pathology and University Pharmacology,* XXVI: 419.

Gould, Peter, and Rodney White. 1974. *Mental Maps.* Harmondsworth, England: Penguin.

Grossman, Gene M., and Alan B. Krueger. 1995. "Economic Growth and the Environment." *The Quarterly Journal of Economics*: 351 – 377.

Hagel, John, and Alvin Roth. 1995. *The Handbook of Experimental Economics.* Princeton, New Jersey: Princeton University Press.

Hall, Robert E., and Charles I. Jones. 1999. "Why Do Some Countries Produce So Much More Output Per Worker than

Others?" *The Quarterly Journal of Economics* CXIV, 1 (February): 83–116.

Hanna, Joël M., Michael A. Little, and Donald M. Austin. 1989. "Climatic Physiology." In *Human Population Biology: A Transdisciplinary Science*, Michael A. Little, and Jere D. Haas, eds. New York: Oxford University Press.

Hellon, R.F. 1975. "Monoamines, Pyrogens and Cations: Their Actions on Central Control of Body Temperature." *Pharmacological Reviews* 26: 289–321.

Hippocrates, Coi. 460 B.C. *The Genuine Works of Hippocrates*, Translated from the Greek, Sydenham Society, London, 1849, by Francis Adams, LLD, Surgeon. Reprinted in Benzinger, Theodor H. ed. 1977. *Temperature: Part I. Arts and Concepts*. Benchmark Papers in Human Physiology. vol. 10. Stroudsburg, PA: Dowden, Hutchinson & Ross.

Hochachka, Peter W., and George N. Somero eds. 1984. *Biochemical Adaptation*. Princeton, NJ: Princeton University Press.

Houdas, Y., and E.F. Ring. 1982. *Human Body Temperature: Its Measurement and Regulation*. New York: Plenum Press.

Howitt, Peter, and Philippe Aghion. 1998. "Capital Accumulation and Innovation As Complementary Factors in Long-Run Growth." *Journal of Economic Growth* 3 (2 June): 111–130.

Huff, W.G. 1994. *The Economic Growth of Singapore: Trade and Development in the Twentieth Century.* Cambridge: Cambridge University Press.

Humphries, Hunter, and Stephen Knowles, 1998, "Does Agriculture Contribute to Economic Growth? Some Empirical Evidence." *Applied Economics* 30: 775–781.

Huntington, E. 1912. "Geographical Environment and Japanese Character." *Journal of Race and Development* II: 256–281.

Isenschmid, R., and L Krehl. 1912. "Uber den Einfluss ges Gehirns auf die Warmeregulation." Naunyn-Schiedeberg's Archive Exp. Patho. Pharmakol., Berlin: Springer-Verlag, 70: 109–134. Reprinted in Benzinger, Theodor H. ed. 1977. *Temperature: Part II. Thermal Homeostasis.* Benchmark Papers in Human Physiology. vol. 10. Stroudsburg, PA: Dowden, Hutchinson & Ross: 57–82.

Islam, Nazrul. 1995. "Growth Empirics: A Panel Data Approach." *The Quarterly Journal of Economics* (November): 1127–1170.

Islam, Nazrul. 1998. "Growth Empirics: A Panel Data Approach—A Reply." *The Quarterly Journal of Economics* (February): 325–329.

Ito, Shinji, Korehiro Ogata, and Hisato Yoshimura. eds. 1972. *Advances in Climatic Physiology.* Tokyo: Igaku Shoin Ltd.

Jacquez, Geoffrey M. 1991. C2D: Spacial Autocorrelation in Two Dimensions. Setauket, New York: Exeter Publishing.

Johnston, Ian A., and Albert F. Bennett. 1996, *Animals and Temperature: Phenotypic and Evolutionary Adaptation*, Society for Experimental Biology, Seminar Series 59, Cambridge: Cambridge University Press.

Jones, Charles I. 1995. "Times Series Test of Endogenous Growth Models." *The Quarterly Journal of Economics* 110 (May): 495−525.

Jones, Charles I. 1997. "Convergence Revisited." *Journal of Economic Growth* 2 (July): 131−154.

Jones, Charles I. 1998. *Introduction to Economic Growth*. W.W. New York: Norton & Company.

Judson, Ruth. 1998. "Economic Growth and Investments in Education: How Allocation Matters." *Journal of Economic Growth* 3 (4 December): 337−360.

Kalat, James W. 1998. *Biological Psychology*. Pacific Grove: Brooks/Cole Publishing Company.

Kaldor, Nicholas. 1961. "Capital Accumulation and Economic Growth." In *Theory of Economic Growth*. Ed. F.A. Lutz and D.C. Hague. New York: St. Martins.

Kangasharju, Aki. 1998. "β Convergence in Finland: Regional Differences in Speed of Convergence." *Applied Economics* 30: 679−687.

Karamarck, Andrew M. 1967. *The Tropics and Economic Development: A Provocative Inquiry into the Poverty of Nations*. Baltimore and London: Johns Hopkins University for the World Bank.

Kates, R.W., and V. Haarmann. 1992. *Environment* 34: 4–11, 25–28.

Kelvin, Lord (W. Thomson). 1848. "On an Absolute Thermometric Scale Founded on Carnot's Theory of the Motive Power of Heat, and Calibrated from Regnault's Observations." *Philosophical Magazine* 33: 313–317.

Keynes, John Maynard. 1923. *Collected writings of John Maynard Keynes*, vol. 4 (a tract on monetary reform), 1971. London: MacMillian.

Knack, Stephen, and Philip Keefer. 1997. "Does Social Capital Have an Economic Payoff? A Cross-Country Investigation," *The Quarterly Journal of Economics* CXII, 3 (November): 1251–1288.

Kremer, Michael. 1993. "Population Growth and Technological Change: 1 Million B.C. to 1990." *Quarterly Journal of Economics*. 108 (August): 681-716.

Krugman, Paul. 1991. *Geography and Trade*. Cambridge, MA: The MIT Press.

Krugman, Paul. 1997. "How Fast Can the U.S. Economy Grow?" *Harvard Business Review* (July-August): 123–129.

Krugman, Paul, and Anthony J. Venables. 1995. "Globalization and the Inequality of Nations." *The Quarterly Journal of Economics* CX 4: 857–880.

Kuznets, Simon. 1971. *Economic Growth of Nations.* Cambridge, MA: Harvard University Press.

Kuznets, Simon. 1973. *Population, Capital and Growth: Selected Essays.* New York: Norton.

Kuznets, Simon. 1966. *Modern Economic Growth.* New Haven: Yale University Press.

Lamb, H.H. 1977. *Climate: Present, Past and Future.* London: Methuen.

Landau, Ralph, Timothy Taylor, and Gavin Wright eds. 1996. *The Mosaic of Economic Growth.* Stanford: Stanford University Press.

Landes, David S. 1998. *The Wealth and Poverty of Nations.* London: Little Brown and Company.

Lavoiser, Antoine Laurent, and Pierre Simon de Laplace. 1782. "Mémoire sur la chaleur." *Histoire de l'Académie Royale des Science,* Paris: 355–373, 393–408. Reprinted in Benzinger, Theodor H. ed. 1977. *Temperature: Part I. Arts and Concepts.* Benchmark Papers in Human Physiology. vol. 10. Stroudsburg, PA: Dowden, Hutchinson & Ross: 145–168.

Lavoisier, Antoine Laurent. 1777. *Mémoire sur la Chaleur*. In *Oeuvres de Lavoisier*, tome II: 1 (1862), Paris.

Lavoisier, Antoine Laurent. 1789. *Traité Elémentaire de Chimie*.

Lee, Kevin, M. Hashem Pesaran, and Ron Smith. 1998. "Growth Empirics: A Panel Data Approach – A Comment." *Quarterly Journal of Economics* 113, 1 (February): 319-323.

Lomax P., E. Schonbaum, and W.L. Veale. 1983. *Environment, Drugs and Thermoregulation*. 5th International Symposium on the Pharmacology of Thermoregulation, Saint-Paul-de-Vence, 1982. Basel: Karger.

Lomax P., E. Schonbaum, and W.L. Veale. 1989 *Thermoregulation: Research and Clinical Applications*. 7th International Symposium on the Pharmacology of Thermoregulation, Odense, 1988. Basel: Karger.

Lucas, Robert E., Jr. 1988. "On the Mechanics of Ecnomic Development." *Journal of Monetary Economics* 22 (July): 3-42.

Macbeth, Helen. 1998. *Food Preferences and Taste*. Providence, RI: Berghahn Books.

Mackowiak, P.A., S.S. Wasserman, and M.M. Levine. 1992. "A Critical Appraisal of 98.6°F, the Upper Limit of Normal Body Temperature, and Other Legacies of Carl Reinhold August Wunderlich." *Journal of the American Medical Association* 268: 1578 – 1580.

Maddison, Angus, and Van der Wee, H. eds. 1994. *Economic Growth and Structural Change: Comparative Approaches Over the Long Run,* Proceedings of the Eleventh International Economic History Congress, Milan, September.

Maddison, Angus (1995), *Monitoring the World Economy.* Paris: Development Center Studies, OECD.

Mankiw, Gregory N. 1997. *Macroeconomics.* New York: Worth Publishers.

Marris, Robin. 1984. "Comparing the Incomes of Nations: A Critique of the International Comparison Project." *Journal of Economic Literature* XXII: 40−57.

Marshall, Alfred. 1949, *Principles of Economics,* 8th ed. chapter I: 59. New York: Porcupine Press.

Mas, M., F. Perez, E. Uriel, and J. Maudos. 1995. "Growth and Convergence in the Spanish Provinces." In *Convergence and Divergence Among European Regions.* H.W. Armstrong, and R.W. Vickerman. eds. *European Research in Regional Science* 5: 66−68.

McArdle, William D., Frank I. Katch, and Victor L. Katch. 1991. *Exercise Physiology: Energy, Nutrition, and Human Performance.* 3d ed. Philadelphia: Lea & Febiger.

McDermott, John. 1997. "Exploitation and Growth." *Journal of Economic Growth* 2, 3 (September): 251−278.

Meadows, Donella H., Dennis L. Meadows, Jorgen Randers, and William W. Hehrens III. 1974. *The Limits to Growth*. New York: Signet.

Mercer, James B. 1989. *Thermal Physiology 1989*. Proceedings of the International Symposium of Thermal Physiology, Tromso, Norway, 16–21 July 1989. Amsterdam: Excerpta Medica.

Meyers, R.D. 1977. "Neurochemical Mechanisms of Two Hypothalmic Temperature Control Systems." In Benzinger, Theodor H. ed. 1977. *Temperature: Part II. Thermal Homeostasis*. Benchmark Papers in Human Physiology. vol. 10. Stroudsburg, PA: Dowden, Hutchinson & Ross: 377–391.

Minier, Jenny A. 1998. "Democracy and Growth: Alternative Approaches." *Journal of Economic Growth* 3, 3 (September): 241–266.

Mitchell, Brian R. 1998. *International Historical Statistics*. Volumes 1 to 3. New York: Stockton Press.

Mitchell, D. 1974. *Physical Basis of Thermoregualtion*. In D. Robertshaw. ed. MTP International Review of Science, Physiology Series One, vol. 7, Environmental Physiology: 1–32. London: Butterworths.

Monteith, J.L. 1973. *Principles of Environmental Physics*. London: Edward Arnold.

Monteith, J.L., and L.E. Mount. 1974. *Heat Loss from Animals and Man*. London: Butterworths.

Montesquieu, C.d. S. d. 1748. *The Spirit of Laws*. Anne M. Cohler, Basia Carolyn Miller, and Harold Samuel Stone. translators. Cambridge, NY: Cambridge University Press, 1989.

Moreno, Ramon, and Bharat Trehan. 1997. "Location and the Growth of Nations." *Journal of Economic Growth* 2 (December): 399–418.

Morgane, Peter J., and Jaak Panksepp. 1980. *Handbook of the Hypothalamus*; vol. 1. Anatomy of the Hypothalamus; vol. 2. Physiology of the Hypothalamus; vol. 3. Behavioral Studies of the Hypothalamus (in two parts). New York: Marcel Dekker. Inc.

Morgenson, G.J., D.L. Jones, and C.Y. Yim. 1980. "From Motivation to Action: Functional Interface between the Limbic System and the Motor System." *Progress in Neurobiology* 14: 69.

Nordhaus, William D. 1994. "Climate and Economic Development." *Proceedings of the World Bank Annual Conference on Development Economics* (1993): 355–376.

Olesen, S., J.J. Bassing, and P.O. Fanger. 1972. "Physiological Comfort Conditions at Sixteen Combinations of Activity, Clothing Air Velocity and Ambient Temperature." *ASHRAE Transactions* 78, 2: 199–206.

Panskepp, Jaak. 1998. *Affective Neuroscience: The Foundations of Human and Animal Emotions* (Series in Affective Science). Oxford: Oxford University Press.

Parker, Philip M. 1995. *Climatic Effects on Individual, Social and Economic Behavior: A Physioeconomic Review of Research Across Disciplines.* Westport, CT: Greenwood Press.

Parker, Philip M. 1997a. *Ethnic Cultures of the World: A Statistical Reference.* Cross-Cultural Statistical Encyclopedia of the World, vol. 3. Westport, CT: Greenwood Press.

Parker, Philip M. 1997b. *Linguistic Cultures of the World: A Statistical Reference.* Cross-Cultural Statistical Encyclopedia of the World, vol. 2. Westport, CT: Greenwood Press.

Parker, Philip M. 1997c. *National Cultures of the World: A Statistical Reference.* Cross-Cultural Statistical Encyclopedia of the World, vol. 4. Westport, CT: Greenwood Press.

Parker, Philip M. 1997d. *Religious Cultures of the World: A Statistical Reference.* Cross-Cultural Statistical Encyclopedia of the World, vol. 1. Westport, CT: Greenwood Press.

Parker, Philip M., and Nader Tavassoli. 1999. "Homeostasis and Consumer Behavior." Working paper. Sloan School of Management, MIT, December.

Perkins. D.W. 1969. *Agricultural Development in China, 1368 – 1968.* Chicago: Aldine.

Persson, J. 1995. "Convergence in Per Capita Income and Migration Across the Swedish Countries 1906—1990." *Institute for International Economic Studies*, Sweden, seminar paper no. 601.

Powles, William E. 1992. *Human Development and Homeostasis: The Science of Psychiatry*. New York: International University Press.

Quah, Danny T. 1993a. "Empirical Cross-Section Dynamics in Economic Growth." *European Economic Review* 37: 426—434.

Quah, Danny T. 1993b. "Galton's Fallacy and Tests of the Convergence Hypothesis." *Scandinavian Journal of Economics* 95: 427—443.

Quah, Danny T. 1996. "Convergence Empirics Across Economies with (Some) Capital Mobility." *Journal of Economic Growth* 1, 1 (March): 95—124.

Quah, Danny T. 1997. "Empirics for Growth and Distribution: Stratification, Polarization, and Convergence Clubs." *Journal of Economic Growth* 2, 1 (March): 27—59.

Raffles, S. 1830. *Memoir of the Life and Public Services of Sir Thomas Stamford Raffles*, Lady Raffles. ed., London: 1830.

Regnier, Philippe. 1991. *Singapore: City-State in South-East Asia*. Honolulu: University of Hawaii Press.

Rhoades, Rodney A., and George A. Tanner. 1995. *Medical Physiology*. Boston: Little, Brown and Company.

Rhodes, Rodney A., and Richard Pflanzer. 1996. *Human Physiology*. 3d ed. Fort Worth: Saunders College Publishing.

Robertshaw, David. ed. 1974. *Environmental Physiology*. vol. 7. Physiology Series One. London: Buttherworths.

Robertshaw, David. ed. 1977. *Environmental Physiology II*. vol. 15. International Review of Physiology. Baltimore: University Park Press.

Robertshaw, David. ed. 1979, *Environmental Physiology III*. vol. 20. International Review of Physiology. Baltimore: University Park Press.

Rodriguez , Francisco, and Jeffrey D. Sachs. 1999. "Why do Resource-Abundant Economies Grow More Slowly." *Journal of Economic Growth* 4, 3 (September): 277-303.

Rolls, Edmund T. 1997. "Neural Processing Underlying Food Selection." In *Food Preferences and Tastes: Community and Change,* Helen Macbeth. ed.: 39–53.

Romer, David. 1996. *Advanced Economics*. New York: McGraw-Hill.

Romer, Paul M. 1989. "Capital Accumulation in the Theory of Long Run Growth." In *Modern Business Cycle Theory*, ed. Robert J. Barro. Cambridge, MA: Harvard University Press.

Rostow, Walt Witman. 1960. *The Stages of Economic Growth.* Cambridge: Cambridge University Press.

Rothman, Tony. 1995. *Instant Physics: from Aristotle to Einstein, and Beyond.* New York: Byron Press.

Rumford, Benjamin, Count of. 1798. "An Inquiry Concerning the Source of Heat which Is Excited by Friction." *Philosophical Transactions of the Royal Society of London.* Part 1, 80–82 and 98–102. Reprinted in Benzinger, Theodor H. ed. 1977. *Temperature: Part I. Arts and Concepts.* Benchmark Papers in Human Physiology. vol. 10. Stroudsburg, PA: Dowden, Hutchinson & Ross: 182–190.

Santinoff, Evelyn. 1980. *Thermoregulation.* Benchmark Papers in Behavior, no. 13, Stroudsburg, PA: Dowden Hutchinson & Ross.

Santorio, Sontorio. 1615. In *Primam Fen Primi Libri Conpis Avicennae*, Venice, 1646: 23–33, and 307–310. Reprinted in Benzinger, Theodor H. ed. 1977. *Temperature: Part I. Arts and Concepts.* Benchmark Papers in Human Physiology. vol. 10. Stroudsburg, PA: Dowden, Hutchinson & Ross: 42–53.

Schumpeter, Joseph A. 1934. *The Theory of Economic Development.* Cambridge, MA: Harvard University Press.

Sen, Amartya. 1977. "Rational Fools: A Critique of the Behavioral Foundations of Economic Theory." *Philosophy and Public Affaires* 6: 317–344.

Sequin, Armand, and Antoine Laurent Lavoiser. 1785. *Premier Mémoire sur La Respiration des Animaux*. Paris: L'Académie Royale des Sciences: 566–584. Translated in English in *Temperature, Part 1: Arts and Concepts*. 1977. Benchmark Papers in Human Physiology, Vol. 9, Benzinger, Theodor H. ed. Stroudsburg, PA: Dowden, Hutchinson & Ross.

Silberberg, Eugene. 1978. *The Structure of Economics: A Mathematical Analysis*. New York: McGraw-Hill Book Company.

Simon, Herbert. 1981. *The Sciences of the Artificial*. Cambridge, MA: The MIT Press.

Smith, Adam. 1776. *An Inquiry into the Nature and Causes of the Wealth of Nations*. London: W. Strahan and T. Cadell.

Solow, Robert M. 1956. "A Contribution to the Theory of Economic Growth." *Quarterly Journal of Economics* 70, 1 (February): 65–94.

Stanier, M.W., L. E. Mount, and J. Bligh. 1984. *Energy Balance and Temperature Regulation*. Cambridge: Cambridge University Press.

Startz, Richard. 1998. "Growth States and Shocks." *Journal of Economic Growth* 3, 3 (September): 203–216.

Stedman, J.D. 1796. *Narrative of a Five Years' Expedition Against the Revolted Negroes of Surinam*, chapter 15 (reprint 1971).

Stiglitz, J. E. 1974. "Growth and Exhaustible Resources: The Competitive Economy." *Review of Economic Studies* (Symposium): 132−152.

Streeten, Paul. 1971. "How Poor Are Poor Countries?" in Seers and Joy, eds. *Development in a Divided World*, Harmondworth, England: Penguin.

Summers, Robert, and Alan Heston. 1991. "The Penn World Table (Mark 5): An Expanded Set of International Comparisons, 1950−1988." *The Quarterly Journal of Economics* 106, 2 (May): 327−368.

Summers, Robert, and Alan Heston. 1993. "Penn World Tables, Version 5.5." Available on diskette. Cambridge, MA: National Bureau of Economic Research.

Temple, Jonathan, and Paul A. Johnson, "Social Capability and Economic Growth." *The Quarterly Journal of Economics* CXIII, 3 (August 1998): 966−990.

Theil, H., and R. Fink. 1983. "The Distance from the Equator As an Instrumental Variable." *Economic Letters* 13: 357−360.

Theil, H., and S. D. Deepak. 1994. "The GDP's of Seven Major Regions, 1950−1990." *Empirical Economics* 19: 517−522.

Theil, H., and J. Glavez. 1995. "On Latitude and Affluence: The Equatorial Grand Canyon." *Empirical Economics* 20: 162−166.

Todardo, Michael P. 1997. *Economic Development*. New York & London: Longman.

Tornell, Aaron. 1997. "Economic Growth and Decline with Endogenous Property Rights." *Journal of Economic Growth* 2, 4 (December): 339–368.

Varian, Hal. 1978. *Microeconomic Analysis*. New York: W.W. Norton & Company.

Ventura, Jaume. 1997. "Growth and Interdependence," *The Quarterly Journal of Economics* CXII, 1 (February).

Vranic, Mladen, Suad Efendic and Charles H. Hollenberg, eds. 1991. *Fuel Homeostasis and the Nervous System*. New York: Plenum.

Wark, Kenneth. 1983. *Thermodynamics*. 4th ed. New York: McGraw-Hill Book Company.

Weber, Max. 1920. "Die protestantische Ethik und der 'Geist' des Kapitalismus." *Archiv fur Sozialwissenschaft u. Sozialpolitik* 20: 1-54; 21: 1-110. Reprinted in *Gesammelte Aufsatze zur Religionssoziologie*. Tubingen: Mohr.

Webster, A.J.F. 1974, "Adaptation to Cold." *Environmental Physiology*, vol. 7, chapter 3, David Robertshaw, ed.: 71–106.

Wenger, C.B., and J. D. Hardy. 1990. "Temperature Regulation and Exposure to Heat and Cold." In Lehmann

J.F. ed.: *Therapeutic Heat and Cold*. 4th ed. Baltimore: Williams & Wilkins: 150−178.

Whittow, G. Causey. 1970. *Comparative Physiology of Thermoregulation*. vol. 1: Invertebrates and Nonmammalian Vertebrates. New York: Academic Press.

Williamson, Phillip, and Richard Moss. 1993. "Degrees of National Wealth." *Nature* 362 (April): 782.

Wilson, Mitchell. 1960. "Count Rumford." *Scientific American* (October): 158.

Winslow, C.E.A., and L.P. Herrington. 1949. *Temperature and Human Life*. Princeton, NJ: Princeton University Press.

Wit, Andrew, and S.C. Wang. 1968. "Temperature-Sensitive Neurons in Pre-optic/anterior Hypothalmic Region: Actions of Pyrogen and Acetylsalicylate." *American Journal of Physiology* 215, 5: 1160−1169.

World Bank. 1999. *World Development Indicators: 1999*. Washington D.C.: The World Bank.

World Heath Organization. 1998. *Obesity: Preventing and Managing the Global Epidemic*. Geneva: World Health Organization.

World Resources Institute. 1998. *World Resources: 1998−1999 Database*. Washington, D.C: World Resources Institute.

Wyndham, C.H., J.F. Morrison, L.D. Holdsworth, C.H. Van Graan, A.J. Van Rensburg, and A. Munro. 1964.

"Physiological Reactions among Cold Caucasian Females." *Journal of Applied Physiology* 19: 877 – 881.

Yoshimura, Hisato, and J. S. Weiner. 1966. *Human Adaptability and its Methodology*. Tokyo: International Council for Scientific Unions by the Japan Society for the Promotion of Sciences.

Yoshimura, M., and H. Yoshimura 1969. "Cold Tolerance and Critical Temperature of Japanese." *International Journal of Biometeorology* 13: 163.

Index